The Christian View of Man

The Christian View of Man

J. GRESHAM MACHEN

The Banner of Truth Trust

THE BANNER OF TRUTH TRUST
3 Murrayfield Road, Edinburgh EH12 6EL
P.O. Box 621, Carlisle, Pennsylvania 17013, USA

★

Copyright THE TRUSTEES u/w J. GRESHAM MACHEN 1937

★

First published in 1937
First Banner of Truth Trust edition 1965
Reprinted 1984
ISBN 0 85151 112 0

★

Printed by McCorquodale (Scotland) Ltd.

Contents

Foreword to British Edition

The Christian View of Man COMPRISES ADDRESSES delivered on the radio by J. Gresham Machen shortly before he departed this life on January 1, 1937. The manuscripts were prepared for publication before his decease but the volume was published posthumously. An earlier series of addresses under the title *The Christian Faith in the Modern World* was published before he died. These two volumes, therefore, represent Dr Machen's maturest thought on the subject of Christian doctrine. He had contemplated at least four such books. But his unexpected demise prevented the accomplishment of this purpose.

The popular style of these two books is explained by the purpose for which the addresses were prepared. Their great value is not thereby diminished; it is enhanced. The literary excellence that characterized all of Dr Machen's writings appears here also. It was his irrepressible virtue to write and speak with the utmost of clarity. Whether he dealt with the difficult questions of scholarly undertaking or the exalted themes of Christian faith no one needed to be in any doubt as to his position nor to struggle in ascertaining his meaning. The spoken and written word was always commensurate with, and the servant of, the precision and logical sequence of his thought. From his first scholarly work, *The Origin of Paul's Religion* (1921), to *The Christian View of Man* completed in the last year of his pilgrimage, this feature stands out as the mark of the ripest and most fruitful scholarship.

Dr Machen's best friends will differ as to what constitutes his greatest work. The choice, however, lies between *The Origin of Paul's Religion* and *The Virgin Birth of Christ* (1930). In both he has shown himself a master in the field of New Testament scholarship, and particularly apologetic. In the defence of the virgin birth there is no work comparable to the latter. In these days when this tenet of the Christian faith is under attack Machen's volume remains as the most thorough and comprehensive vindication of its biblical basis and of the indispensable place it occupies in the grand miracle of the Incarnation.

There are two other books of somewhat different character from the four already mentioned. They are *Christianity and Liberalism* (1923), in which the thesis is that 'liberalism' is a distinct religion proceeding from an entirely different root from that of the faith of the historic Christian church, and *What is Faith?* (1925). The theme of the latter is similar to that of *Christianity and Liberalism,* but its central purpose was to combat the anti-intellectualism of the modernism of that period. In so doing, however, Machen also expounded more positively the nature of faith and various aspects of Christian doctrine.

These two books are an index to other phases of Machen's character and witness. Masterful scholar as he was he was no recluse. *Christianity and Liberalism* shows his burning zeal to vindicate the distinctive character of the Christian faith against all counterfeit. But his labours to this end were not confined to the literary sphere. From the early nineteen-twenties he became deeply involved in the controversies concerned with the great issues of the faith in his own denomination, the Presbyterian Church in the U.S.A., and in other Churches on the North American continent. Though in this conflict Dr Machen's pen was constantly at work and was his most effective instrument, yet his devotion to Christ and his profound jealousy for Christ's honour in the church made it morally impossible for him to stand aside and be a spectator in the areas of practical life in the church. He had no love for ecclesiastical conflict. The record shows how reluctant he was to enter upon such activity. But his sense of presbyterial responsibility was acute and when great issues were at stake the claims of Truth and of Christ his Lord left no other alternative. Without any wavering or relaxation of effort he gave himself with his whole soul to those causes designed to preserve and proclaim the truth of God's Word in its integrity and to maintain the church of Christ in its purity and glory.

J. Gresham Machen's contendings were the occasion for much misunderstanding, misrepresentation, hostility and persecution. This is the lot of every faithful witness and the cost of fidelity. Though a man of intense loyalty in his friendships, he never allowed human friendship to mar or compromise his supreme loyalty to Christ. With weakness or vacillation in the cause of Truth he had no sympathy, and his severity of rebuke was after the pattern of the apostle to whose life and teaching he had devoted so much study. But, in the words of his biographer who had been his colleague and then successor in the department of New Testament at Westminster Theological Seminary, 'If ever there was a man of nobility, magnanimity, gentility and tender considerateness, Machen was that man' (Ned B. Stonehouse: *J. Gresham Machen: A Biographical Memoir*, Grand Rapids, 1955, p. 327). Severity and tenderness were not antithetical; they were complementary after the model of our supreme example, the Saviour Himself. Of

Bunyan's characters Dr Machen was Valiant-for-Truth and in Bunyan's poetic terms:

> 'Who would true valour see,
> Let him come hither;
> One here will constant be,
> Come wind, come weather.'

JOHN MURRAY

February, 1965

Author's Preface

THIS BOOK CONSTITUTES THE SECOND PART OF A series of radio addresses which the author has been delivering over station WIP, under the auspices of Westminster Theological Seminary, Philadelphia. The first part, which was published in February, 1936, under the title *The Christian Faith in the Modern World*, dealt with the authority of the Bible and with the Biblical doctrine of God. The present volume deals with the Biblical doctrine of man, including the related subjects of the decrees of God and predestination. A considerable part of the discussion is concerned with what the Bible says about sin.

The book does not pretend in the slightest to be original. It is dependent throughout upon the masters of the Reformed Theology – particularly upon Charles Hodge, A. A. Hodge, B. B. Warfield, and Geerhardus Vos – and grateful acknowledgment is also due to Caspar Wistar Hodge, of whom, as of Warfield and Vos, the author was formerly a pupil. The author believes that the Reformed Faith should be preached, as well as taught in the classroom, and that the need for the preaching of it is particularly apparent at the present time. The author is trying to preach it in this little book, and preach it very specifically to the people of our generation.

The book is not, indeed, a collection of sermons. Its several chapters proceed in logical sequence and seek to develop one central theme. But it does seek to show that the Reformed doctrine of man, and particularly the Reformed doctrine of sin and grace, is not something useful merely to the theologian but a matter of the most vital concern to every man.

Grateful acknowledgment is again made to the Rev. Edwin H. Rian, of the Board of Trustees of Westminster Seminary, to whom the initiation and continuance of the radio addresses is due. The author is grateful also to his colleagues in the Faculty of Westminster Theological Seminary, whose wise counsel and generous assistance have been of great value at a number of points.

J. GRESHAM MACHEN

1: The Living and True God

AS WE BEGIN TO CONSIDER THE CHRISTIAN VIEW OF man, with the decrees of God which underlie man's existence, we certainly find ourselves in the midst of a troubled world. We are living certainly today in a time of rapid changes. Less than twenty years after a war that was supposed to have been fought to make the world safe for democracy, democracy almost everywhere is lying prostrate, and liberty is rapidly being destroyed. Who would have thought, twenty years ago, that within so short a period of time all freedom of speech and of the press would have been destroyed in large sections of western Europe? Who would have thought that Europe would sink back so soon into a worse than medieval darkness?

America has been no exception to this decadence. Liberty is being threatened, and there is coming up before us in the near future the spectre of the hopeless treadmill of a collectivistic state.

Certainly when we take the world as a whole, we are obliged to see that the foundations of liberty and honesty are being destroyed, and the slow achievements of centuries are being thrown recklessly away.

In such a time of kaleidoscopic changes, is there anything that remains unchanged? When so many things have proved to be untrustworthy, is there anything that we can trust?

One point, at least, is clear – we cannot trust the Church. The visible Church, the Church as it now actually exists upon this earth, has fallen too often into error and sin.

No, we cannot appeal from the world to the Church.

Well, then, is there anything at all to which we can appeal? Is there anything at all that remains constant when so many things change?

I have a very definite answer to give to that question. It is contained in a verse taken from the prophecy of Isaiah: 'The grass withereth, the flower fadeth: but the word of our God shall stand forever.' There are many things that change, but there is one thing that does not change. It is the Word of the living and true God. The world is in decadence, the visible Church is to a considerable extent apostate; but when God speaks we can trust Him, and His Word stands forever sure.

Where has God spoken? Where shall we find that Word of God? I tried to give the answer in the first part of this series of talks, which has appeared under the title of *The Christian Faith in the Modern World*. We can find the Word of God in the Bible. We do not say merely that the Bible contains the Word of God; we say that the Bible is the Word of God. In a time of turmoil and distress, and in the perplexity and weakness of our own lives, we can turn with perfect confidence to that blessed Book.

When we say that the Bible is the Word of God, we mean something very definite indeed. We mean that the Bible is true. We mean that the writers of the Bible, in addition to all their providential qualifications for their task, received an immediate and supernatural guidance and impulsion of the Spirit of God which kept them from the errors that are found in other books, and made the resulting book, the Bible, to be completely true in what it says regarding matters of fact, and completely authoritative in its commands. That is the great doctrine of the full or plenary inspiration of Holy Scripture.

That doctrine does not, as is so often charged, do violence to the individuality of the Biblical writers; and it does not mean that they became mere automata without knowledge of what they were doing. But it does mean that the work of the Holy Spirit in inspiration was a supernatural work. It was not a mere work of God's providence; it was not a mere employment by God of the resources of the universe that He had made: but it was a gracious interposition into the course of nature by the immediate power of God.

That doctrine means that the Bible is God's book, not man's book. Other books give advice that is good and advice that is bad; this book gives only advice that is good, or rather it issues commands that come with the full authority of the sovereign God.

It is upon that high view of the Bible that the present series of talks is based. I am going to seek to explore the Bible with you in order to see what God, and not merely man, has said.

In that presentation of what God has told us in the Bible I hope indeed not to be without sympathy for the man who does not believe as I believe; I hope not to be without sympathy for the man who has doubts. I hope to be able to show such a man as I go along that some of the objections to the teaching of the Bible which are current among men today are based upon misunderstanding of what the Bible means or upon a failure to consider important confirmatory evidence of the Bible's truth. But all that should not obscure what I am trying to do. I am not trying to present to you things that I have discovered for myself, and I am not trying to help you to discover things for yourselves; but I am asking you to listen with me to what God has told us in His Word.

In the series of which the present series is the continuation, I made a beginning of talking to you about what God has told us in His Word.

The revelation of God which is contained in the Bible, we observed, is not the only revelation that God has given. God has revealed Himself through the universe that He has made. 'The heavens declare the glory of God, and the firmament sheweth his handywork.' He has also revealed Himself through His voice within us, the voice of conscience. 'When the Gentiles that have not the law do by nature the things contained in the law, these, having not the law, are a law unto themselves.' The Bible puts the stamp of its approval upon what may be called 'natural religion'.

But the revelation of God through nature is not the only revelation that God has given. In addition to it He has given a revelation that is called 'supernatural' because it is above nature.

Such supernatural revelation was needed for two reasons.

In the first place, the revelation of God through nature had become hidden from men's eyes through sin. The wonders of God's world ought to have made men worship and glorify the Creator, but their foolish heart was darkened. The voice of conscience ought to have told plainly what is right and what is wrong, but men's conscience had become seared as with a hot iron. So a new and plain confirmation of what nature and conscience said was needed by sinful man.

In the second place – and this is even more important to observe – man as sinner needed to have revealed to Him about God certain things of which nature and conscience provided no slightest hint. He needed to have revealed to him the grace of God. He was not only blinded by sin, but he was lost in sin. He was under its guilt and curse. He was under its power. He needed to be told the way in which God had saved him. Nature said nothing whatever about that. Knowledge of that could come to sinful man only in a way which was in the strictest sense supernatural.

How wonderfully rich is that supernatural revelation as it is found in the Bible! How far it transcends the revelation of God through nature! The whole doctrine of the Trinity, the whole appearance and work of the Lord Jesus Christ, the entire application of the work of Christ to the believer through the Holy Spirit, the whole glorious promise of a world to come – these things are not told us through nature; they are told us in the Bible and in the Bible alone. They are told us by a revelation that is not natural but supernatural.

In the previous series, I made a beginning of talking to you about that revelation. I talked to you about the great Biblical doctrine of the Triune God. There is but one God, but God is in three persons – Father, Son and Holy Ghost.

At the heart of that establishment in the Bible of the doctrine of the Trinity, we saw, is the teaching of the Bible regarding the deity of Jesus Christ.

Some nineteen hundred years ago, there lived in Palestine a certain person, Jesus.

There are two opinions about Him.

Some regard Him simply as a great religious genius, the founder of one of the world's great religions, a man who kept His own person out of His gospel, did not ask that men should have any particular opinion about Him but simply proclaimed to them the Father God, asked not that men should have faith in Him but only that they should have faith in God like the faith which He had in God. According to those who hold that view Jesus was

[17]

simply a teacher and example, the pathfinder for mankind on the way to God. That view is the view of unbelievers.

But there is another view of Jesus. According to that other view, the person known to history as Jesus of Nazareth existed from all eternity. He was infinite – eternal and unchangeable God. It was through Him that this vast universe was made. He came into this world by His own voluntary act. He took upon Himself our nature, being born as a man in order that He might redeem His people on the cross. When He was on earth, He offered Himself to men as the object of their faith, not asking them merely to have faith in God like the faith which He had in God, but asking them to have faith in Him. Upon faith in Him he made salvation to depend. He died on the cross as a sacrifice to satisfy divine justice and reconcile us to God. He rose from the dead. He is God and man in two distinct natures and one person forever. He will come again and we shall see Him. He will come again and we shall see Him with our very eyes. This view of Jesus is the view of Christians.

We saw that that Christian view of Jesus is the view that is taught in the Bible, and that it is the view that Jesus taught regarding Himself.

Did Jesus really present Himself when He was on earth merely as an example for men's faith? Did He say merely: 'Have faith in God like the faith which I have in God'? Was He indifferent to what men thought of Him?

These questions are easy to answer if we take the Bible record of Jesus as a whole. The Jesus who is presented in the Bible as a whole clearly offered Himself to men as the object of their faith, and made faith in Him essential to the attaining of eternal life.

But unbelievers will not accept the Bible record of Jesus

as a whole. Very well, then, I will say to an unbelieving friend: 'Here is a New Testament. Take it and choose any passage in it that you will in order to prove that your view of Jesus is right. You do not like my passages. Well, let us see what your passages say.'

We observed in our last series of talks that there is one passage which an unbeliever is more likely to choose when so challenged than any other. It is the passage called the Sermon on the Mount. There, it is said by unbelievers, we have a non-theological Jesus, a Jesus who issued lofty commands and supposed that those commands could be obeyed no matter what men thought of Him. We are constantly told that. Theology, we are told, is not the important thing, even the theology that deals with Jesus Christ. If, we are told, men would just get up and do what Jesus says in the Sermon on the Mount, that would be far better than coming to any particular opinion about Him or about the meaning of His death.

'Well,' I will just say to such an unbelieving friend, 'let us just take that passage which you have chosen, let us just take that Sermon on the Mount, to see whether it really bears out your view of Jesus, whether it really presents to us a Jesus who was merely a teacher and example and did not ask men to have any particularly high view of Him.'

We did that in our last series. We took the Sermon on the Mount to examine it in that way. And what did we find? Did we find a Jesus who kept His own person out of His gospel and did not care what men thought of Him?

Most emphatically we did not. Instead, we found in the Sermon on the Mount a Jesus who in the most amazing way dispensed the rewards in the Kingdom of God, a Jesus who placed His commands fully on an equality with the commands of God in the Old Testament Scriptures, a Jesus who did not say as the prophets said, 'Thus saith the Lord,' but who said, '*I* say to you,' a Jesus who pronounced blessedness upon the men who stood in a certain relation to Him – 'Blessed are ye when men shall revile you and persecute you and say all manner of evil against you falsely *for my sake*' – a Jesus who claimed that He would one day sit on the judgment seat of God and determine the final destinies of men, sending some into everlasting punishment and others into eternal life.

No, we cannot in the Sermon on the Mount find any escape from the Christ of the rest of the New Testament. We cannot find in that passage – favourite passage of unbelievers though it be – any merely human Jesus who was indifferent to what men thought of Him and merely asked them to take Him as their example and to follow His leading on the pathway to God. We find in that passage as in every other passage one Christ and one Christ only – the Christ who was truly man and truly God.

If, moreover, we did find in the New Testament the Christ that some men are seeking, a mere leader and example, a mere explorer of the pathway which leads men to God, what possible good could such a Christ be to our souls? What possible good could a mere example and guide be to those who, like us, are dead in trespasses and sins and are under the just wrath and curse of God?

I remember that several years ago I addressed a meeting here in Philadelphia that was devoted to a consideration of the topic 'The Responsibility of the Church in Our New Age'. One of the speakers, who was not a Christian – I mean not even a professing Christian at all – had some very kind things to say about Jesus. But the climax of his address came when he quoted Jesus' words from the Old Testament regarding love of God and of one's neighbour:

'Thou shalt love the Lord thy God with all thy heart, and with all thy soul, and with all thy mind, and thou shalt love thy neighbour as thyself.'

'Is that not dogma enough for anybody?' said the speaker.

Well, of course, it is not dogma at all, or doctrine, but a command. But was the speaker right in holding that it is large enough for anybody; and if he was right in holding that it is large enough for anybody, why do we Christians insist on adding to it extensive doctrines including the doctrine of the deity of Christ? Why do we not just content ourselves with saying, 'Thou shalt love the Lord thy God, and thou shalt love thy neighbour as thyself'? Is that not indeed large enough for anybody?

What is the answer from the Christian point of view? The answer from the Christian point of view is very simple. Yes, certainly that great double command of Jesus, 'Thou shalt love the Lord thy God with all thy heart, and with all thy soul, and with all thy mind, and thou shalt love thy neighbour as thyself' is plenty large enough for anybody. Ah, but do you not see, my friends, it is far too large. There is the whole trouble. That is the whole reason why we are Christians. That stupendous command of Jesus is too large; it is so large that we have not succeeded in keeping it. If we had loved God and our neighbour, in the high sense in which Jesus meant that command, all would have been well with us; we should then have needed nothing more; we should not have needed any doctrine of the Cross of Christ because we should not have needed any cross of Christ; we should not have needed any doctrine of the person of Christ – God and man in two distinct natures and one person forever – because there would have been no necessity for Christ to become man at all. We should have been righteous, and should have needed no Saviour.

But as it is we are sinners. That is the reason why we need more than a teacher and example and lawgiver; that is the reason why we need what unbelievers despise as being merely doctrine and we prefer to call the gospel; that is why we cling with all our souls to the great Bible doctrines of the person and work of Jesus Christ.

Suppose I had listened to Jesus merely as a great example and lawgiver. Suppose I had heard Him say, 'Thou shalt love the Lord thy God and thy neighbour as thyself'; suppose I had heard Him say, in the Sermon on the Mount, 'Blessed are the pure in heart; for they shall see God.' What should I say to Him then? Should I say: 'I thank you, Jesus; that is all I needed to know; I am so glad to know that if I love God and my neighbour and am pure in heart all will be well and I shall enter the Kingdom of God.'

Well, my friends, I do not know what you would say. But I know that I could say nothing of the kind. I could only say, after listening to those commands of Jesus: 'Alas, I am undone; I have not loved God and my neighbour; I am not pure in heart; I am a sinner; Jesus, have you anything, despite your high commands, to say to me?'

When I come thus to Jesus as a sinner, confessing that I have not obeyed His commands, confessing that I have nothing to offer to Him, but am utterly unworthy and utterly helpless, has He anything to say to me? Does He say merely: 'You have heard my high commands; that is all that I have to say; that is all the gospel that I have to give you; that is all the doctrine you can have.'

No, thank God, that is not all that He has to give me – that cold comfort of a command that I have not kept and cannot keep. He gives me something more than that. He gives me Himself. He offers Himself to me in the Bible as my Saviour who died for me on the Cross and who now lives as the one whom I can trust. He offers Himself to me in the great doctrines of His person and His work. If He were some other, He could not save me and I could not trust Him to save me. But because He is very God, He could save me and did save me and I have been united to Him by the Holy Spirit through faith.

Do you not see, my friends? That is the reason why the Christian clings to the doctrine of the deity of Christ. He does not approach it as a cold academic matter, but he comes to it as a drowning man lays hold of a plank that may save him from the abyss. No lesser Christ could save us; this Christ alone could save us from eternal death.

It is in that way that we are going to approach the things that we hope to deal with in the talks that follow. The doctrine presented in the Bible is not to us just a matter of curious interest; it is not a thing to be relegated to schools or classrooms. It is a matter of tragic import; it is a matter of life or death. Here we stand on the brink of eternity. We are sinners. We deserve God's wrath and curse. There is hope for us only in what God has told us in His Word. Let us listen to it while there is time.

2: The Decrees of God

IN A FORMER SERIES OF TALKS,[1] I SPOKE TO YOU about what God is. Now I want to begin to talk to you about what God does.

But before we speak about *what* God does, the first question to ask is whether God can really do anything at all. There are many ways of thinking about God that really deny to Him the power to act altogether. If, for example, God is just a blind force, or just another name for the universe as a whole, or if He is merely a name for one aspect of the universe, or a mere symbol to express the highest aspirations of humanity, then it is only by a very loose use of language that He can be said to act. Strictly speaking only persons act, and when we come to talk about God as acting, we do so only because we reject all impersonal conceptions of Him and regard Him, as the Bible does, clearly as a person.

Since God is a person, He is free. Freedom is a characteristic of personality. A machine is not free; a current flowing downward in a groove fixed for it is not free; a plant is not free. But a person is free to act or not to act, and he is free to act in this way or in that. Since God is a person He also is free. Indeed, He is free to an extent to which no finite person is free.

But when we say that God is free it is very important that we should understand exactly what we mean and what we do not mean.

Do we mean that His actions are quite uncertain, so that

[1] See *The Christian Faith in the Modern World*, 1936.

it is always impossible to be sure beforehand whether He will act or how He will not act? Do we mean that His will is a sort of balance which may swing this way or may swing that way without any rhyme or reason? Do we mean that there is nothing at all to which His actions conform, or by which they are bound?

I think a little reflection will show that we cannot possibly mean that. If we did mean that we should be obliged to say that God might break His covenant with His people or do any other base deed. But if one thing is certain above all else it is that God will never do anything of that kind. I think it is not wrong to say that He *cannot* do anything of that kind.

Why can He not do such things? Because there is any external compulsion upon Him not to do them? Because if He does them His doing of them will anywhere be called in question? Most assuredly not. There is no compulsion of any kind resting upon God; He is absolutely sovereign; He can do just exactly as He wills; there is none who can say to Him, 'What doest thou?'

Yet it is entirely certain, where a good action is being contemplated in comparison with a bad one, that He will choose the good and reject the bad. In fact, there is nothing at all that is more certain than that. It is upon that certainty that all other certainties depend. It is absolutely impossible that God should do wrong.

Why is it impossible? Surely the answer is plain. It is impossible for Him to do wrong because for Him to do wrong would be contrary to His own nature. 'God is a Spirit, infinite, eternal, and unchangeable, in His being, wisdom, power, holiness, justice, goodness, and truth.' Those are His attributes; without those attributes He would not be God; those attributes determine all His actions.

[25]

Never in the very smallest of all His works will He depart by one hair's breadth from that perfect standard which the perfection of His own nature sets up.

I think that is what one of my old teachers meant when he said, if I remember rightly his words, that God is the most obligated being that there is. He is obligated by His own nature. He is infinite in His wisdom; therefore He can never do anything that is unwise. He is infinite in His justice; therefore He can never do anything that is unjust. He is infinite in His goodness; therefore He can never do anything that is not good. He is infinite in His truth; therefore it is impossible that He should lie.

Even a man's actions are somewhat similarly determined. They spring from the nature of the man. Experience surely teaches that. But the Bible teaches it most clearly of all. A 'good tree cannot bring forth evil fruit, neither can a corrupt tree bring forth good fruit'. A man's choices are free in the sense that they are not just determined by external compulsion. But they are not free if by freedom is meant freedom from determination by the man's own character.

So it is also in the case of the supreme Person, God. His actions are free in the sense that they are not determined by anything external to Him. But they certainly are determined by His own nature. They will always be holy and they will always be just and good, because He is holy and just and good.

Indeed, the actions of God are even more completely determined by His own nature than a man's actions are determined by *his* own nature. A man's actions spring from his nature. Yes, but the man's nature may be changed; God can change it. But in the case of God no such possibility of change exists; God is infinite, eternal *and unchangeable*.

[26]

Never, never, never, therefore – never by the remotest possibility can He perform an action which is not holy, wise and powerful, just and good and true.

His actions, therefore, are more free than the actions of finite persons, and at the same time more directly determined than the actions of finite persons. They are more free than the actions of finite persons because never, either directly or indirectly, can they be determined by anything external to the Person Himself, as is possible in the case of finite persons; and they are more directly determined than the actions of finite persons because never by any possibility can there be any change in that nature of the Person Himself.

Thus it is very important for us to observe that the freedom of God's actions does not mean that they can by any possibility be out of accord with God's nature.

But there is another thing also which it is very important to observe that the freedom of God's actions does not mean. It does not mean that they are purposeless actions; it does not mean that they are undetermined by ends which God has in view.

At this point also, there is a real analogy between the freedom of God and the freedom of finite persons. Take the finite person with whom we are most familiar – namely, man. Does the freedom of a man's will mean that a man acts independently of motives? Does it mean that when a man chooses to do one thing rather than to do another thing his choice is determined by nothing at all except just that it is his choice? Well, some people have apparently thought that that is the case. But surely these people are wrong. Surely the actions of a person, just because they are free actions, and not mere meaningless vagaries of blind chance, are determined by motives. When a man is placed before some important turning-point in his life, he sets before himself the considerations on one side and then the considerations on the other side, and then in the light of those considerations, of the preponderance on the one side or on the other, he acts. It is just that operation of motives in determining the man's action that makes the action a truly personal action and so makes it in the right sense of the word a 'free' action.

If then a finite person, man, in his truly personal actions, is determined by motives, something like that is also true of the infinite Person, God. God also has ends in view when He acts. His will must not be thought of as though it were swinging blindly in a sort of vacuum, without relation to His infinite knowledge and wisdom. No, the choices of God's will are always – not sometimes, but always – determined by the ends which His infinite knowledge and His infinite wisdom place before Him.

A denial of that view of the will – a denial, that is, of the view that truly personal actions are not the actions of an undetermined will, but of a will determined by motives or ends – is sometimes represented as though it were in the interests of freedom. How can a person really be free, it is said, if his actions are fixed by something other than his will itself at the moment when he makes his choice? How can a person be free if he cannot act irrespectively of the ends that he has in view?

But a little reflection will show that the exact opposite is the case. If a man's choices are not determined by the ends that he has in view, but simply by meaningless oscillations of his will, then they are determined by nothing but chance and the man becomes the mere plaything of something external to himself.

That is particularly clear in the case of the supreme Person, God. If God's choices were not determined at all times by the holy ends that He has in view, if His will swung this way or that without reference to anything save His will itself, considered as though it were separate from His knowledge and wisdom, then His actions could only be regarded as dependent upon a blind meaningless chance; and in that case they would cease to be really personal actions and God would cease to be God.

No, we must really hold to a sound determinism when we think of the will. The will of man is not free in the sense that it operates independently of the feelings and the intellect. Indeed, if we regard the will as a sort of separate somewhat inside of a man, going about its business in its own way, capable of taking advice from other parts of man's nature but also capable of acting quite independently of such advice when the mood strikes it – if we think of the will thus, we are getting very far away from reality indeed. We are really making of something that we call the will a little separate personality; we are doing away with the unity of the man's personality. As a matter of fact, there is really no such thing as the will out of relation to the other aspects of the person. What we call the will is just the whole person making choices.

With regard to the infinite Person, God, we have to speak differently in important respects from the way in which we speak of finite persons. Yet of Him, as of the finite persons whom He has created, it does remain true that when He wills to do something, He wills to do it because of ends that He has in view. His actions are not the chance swingings hither and yon of something within Him that can be called His will, but they are the actions of the majestic unity of His being, and they are determined by high and holy ends.

I do not mean that when God wills to do something *we* can always see what the end is. On the contrary, in countless cases, we can only see that it is His will, and that should be enough for us. We are sure that whatever He does is done with a holy purpose. The purpose is often hidden in the mystery of the divine wisdom. For us to refuse to bow to God's will just because we do not know what His purpose is – that is the very height of irreligion. It is the sin of all sins; it is to pit our ignorance against His infinite wisdom and knowledge; it is rebellion and pride and madness. May God save us all from such a sin as that!

Yet although we have no *right* to know what God's purposes are, He has in His wonderful goodness been pleased to lift here and there the veil that hides His counsels from our eyes. With what reverence ought we to look into the mysteries within the veil! With what reverence ought we to approach the holy Book in which those mysteries are revealed!

We have spoken of the purposes of God. The theologians when they speak of them call them His decrees.

How many are there of such decrees? An infinite number, we might be tempted to say. How manifold are the manifestations of God's goodness in our own lives! And when we think of the vastness of the universe and the countless ages, we naturally say that the decrees of God are beyond anything that by any possibility can be numbered.

If we say that, we are saying something that is profoundly true; and yet when we look at the matter a little more closely and more deeply, there is a true sense in which we can say that the purposes of God, infinite in number though they may seem to be, are all just one purpose, are all just portions or aspects of one great plan.

That is what the Shorter Catechism means when it says that the decrees of God are 'His eternal purpose'. It is not by chance that the singular number of the word 'purpose' is there used. The many decrees all constitute just one purpose or one plan. They are not without relation to one another, but form a mighty unity as God Himself is one.

You will notice that the Shorter Catechism speaks of that purpose as an eternal purpose. 'The decrees of God,' it says, 'are His *eternal* purpose.' What does it mean by that? Well, it means something that it is very important indeed for us to observe, and it means something which is close to the heart of what the Bible teaches.

The Bible does often speak of the decrees of God as though they came one after another, in an order of time. Indeed, the Bible sometimes uses some very bold language about these matters. It speaks even of God's repenting of what He has done. For instance, it says that 'it repented the Lord that he had made man';[1] and that 'the Lord repented that he had made Saul king over Israel.'[2] These passages might seem to a superficial reader, if they were taken by themselves, to mean that God makes many decrees, at many different times, and as though the decrees were widely different from one another.

But that would be a very superficial interpretation of those passages. When we look a little more closely we see plainly what the Bible means. When it speaks of God as repenting of something that He has done, it is looking at the thing from the point of view of men who are living in a succession of time upon this earth. God does one thing at one time, and one thing at another. He made man, and then, when man had sinned, He destroyed man, with the exception of the few whom He preserved

[1] Gen. 6:6.   [2] 1 Sam. 15:35.

alive. He made Saul king, and then removed him from being king. Looked at from the point of view of the execution of God's decrees, it is as though God's decrees or purposes had changed; and the Bible makes that clear in simple language drawn from the ordinary life of men. But it is also perfectly clear that the Bible does not mean such language to be taken literally as though it meant that God was surprised in the way in which a man would be surprised, or as though it meant that the plans of God are shifted as a man's plans are shifted to meet developments over which he has no control.

At this point it is possible that I may be met with an objection. 'There you are,' the objector may say, 'you miserable believers in the inspiration of the Bible are up to your old tricks. When you find anything in the Bible that you like, you insist on taking it with a most distressing literalness; but when you find anything that you do not like, you crawl out of it, as in the present case, by saying that figurative language is being used.'

Such is the objection. But, do you know, my friends, I am not so very much dismayed by it. I think I have a perfectly good answer to it. 'Yes,' I would say to the objector, 'I do take some things in the Bible literally and some things figuratively. But I have a perfectly good reason for doing so. I have a perfectly good way of deciding which things in the Bible I shall take literally and which things I shall take figuratively. It is not that I take those things literally which I like and explain away those things as figurative which I do not like; but I take those things literally which the Bible intends literally and those things figuratively which the Bible intends figuratively.'

You see, I hold that the Bible is essentially a plain book. Common sense is a wonderful help in reading it. I am not forgetting that the enlightening of the eyes which the Holy Spirit gives in the new birth is necessary in order that sinful man may really lay hold upon the central message in the Bible; but sometimes I am tempted to say that one of the most obvious effects of the new birth should be the restoration of plain common sense in the understanding of the perfectly plain utterances of Holy Scripture. So I submit that if a man really reads with ordinary good sense and good will those utterances of the Bible where the Bible speaks of God as repenting of the things that He has done, and the like, he will have no difficulty whatever in seeing that those passages are most emphatically not to be interpreted literally and that a literal interpretation of them is a very heinous exhibition of misunderstanding and bad taste.

Such anthropomorphic language – if you will permit me to use a long word – sets forth an important truth. It teaches us that God deals with us as a living person deals with us. He follows our actions and the changing circumstances of our lives, and His actions are related to changes in our actions and in our circumstances. The Bible sets that forth by the use of the language of which we have been speaking.

But the Bible also very plainly teaches us that when we look at the depth of this matter we must see that the purpose of God, which is executed in His infinitely varied dealings with mankind and with the universe in an order of time, is itself quite out of anything like a temporal succession. There is no before and no after to God. He really created time, indeed, when He created finite beings, and time, like the rest of the universe which God created, is not a mere appearance, but has a real existence. But to God all things are eternally present.

So the Shorter Catechism is right when it says that the decrees of God are His *eternal* purpose. I think that really runs all through the Bible. It is not obscured a bit by the simple, anthropomorphic language about which we have spoken this afternoon. At times it comes into particularly plain view, as when the Bible says in the first chapter of Ephesians that God chose us in Christ before the creation of the world. But what ought to be emphasized above all else is that the doctrine of an eternal purpose of God is the foundation upon which all the teaching of the Bible is really based. Back of all the events of human history, back of all the changes in the inconceivable vastness of the universe, back of space itself and time, there lies one mysterious purpose of Him to whom there is no before or after, no here or yonder, to whom all things are present and before whom all things are naked and open, the living and holy God.

3: God's Decrees and Man's Freedom

THE DECREES OF GOD, WE HAVE OBSERVED, MAY BE thought of as many, if we look at them from the point of view of their execution in the infinitely varied course of God's dealings with the world that He has made; but it is a still profounder truth to say that they are all really one decree, one eternal purpose or plan.

How much is embraced in that eternal purpose of God?

The true answer to that question is very simple. The true answer is 'Everything'. Everything that happens is embraced in the eternal purpose of God; nothing at all happens outside of His eternal plan.

It is obvious that nothing is too great for God. The stupendous spaces of the universe, which astronomers talk of in terms of light-years but of which neither they nor any of the rest of us can really form any conception at all, contain no mysteries for God. He made all and He rules all, and all is embraced in His eternal purpose.

It is equally clear that nothing is too small for God. Jesus expressed that truth with a vividness that can never be surpassed. 'Are not two sparrows,' He said, 'sold for a farthing? and one of them shall not fall on the ground without your Father. But the very hairs of your head are all numbered.'[1] No, nothing is too trivial to form a part of God's eternal plan. That plan embraces the small as well as the great.

Modern science has disclosed new wonders in the starry heavens, and it has also told us of the infinitesimal universe

[1] Matt. 10:29 f.

that the atom contains. Well, it is all naked and open before God, and it all is the product of His infinite wisdom and power.

But wait a moment. We said that everything that happens is embraced in God's eternal plan, being determined from all eternity in one majestic purpose. Did we really mean that? When we said 'Everything', did we really mean 'Everything'? Did we allow no exceptions? Is everything fixed and determined in God's plan? Is there nothing at all that is free?

How about, then, the free actions of personal beings such as man? Is not man's freedom of choice a delusion if all is fixed in God's eternal plan?

There are those who have been impressed by this objection and have actually regarded the personal choices of persons, especially man, as lying outside the range of the things that are fixed in God's eternal purpose. When God created persons, they have said, He left the persons free; otherwise they would not have been persons at all. So, they have said, God voluntarily refrains from using His omnipotence so far as the actions of His personal creatures are concerned. He was powerful enough as Creator even to create beings with the mysterious gift of free will. He then stands aside and lets those beings exercise that mysterious gift. Their actions in detail, therefore – so the argument runs – are not fixed in God's eternal plan but are dependent upon that mysterious power of choice which God gave them once for all.

This view may be held in two forms. In the first place, those who hold it may say that God does not even know beforehand what choices the persons whom He has created will make; and in the second place, they may say that God knows beforehand what choices the persons whom He has created will make but simply does not determine those choices; He foreknows those choices but does not fore-ordain them; He knows what things His creatures will do but does not secure their doing of them.

The former of these two forms of the theory seems to do away with the omniscience of God. Whatever may or may not be said of the possibility that God should voluntarily refrain from using His omnipotence, it is quite clear that to say that He refrains from possessing His omniscience is simply to indulge in a contradiction in terms. If God really knows all things, then He knows what His creatures, including man, will do. I really do not see how we can get away from that.

If God does not know what His creatures, including man, will do, then a wild, unaccountable factor is introduced into the universe. Can that unaccountable factor be isolated? Can we hold that although God does not know what the persons whom He has created will do, yet He can go on governing the rest of the universe in an orderly fashion? Surely we cannot hold that at all. No, there is a marvellous concatenation in the course of the world; one part cannot possibly be isolated from the rest in that fashion. If God does not know what the personal beings in the universe will do, then the whole course of the world is thrown into confusion. The order of nature then ceases to be an order at all.

God, moreover, on that view, ceases to be God. He becomes a being who has to wait to see what His creatures will do; He becomes a God who has to change His plans to meet changing circumstances. In other words, He becomes a God who stands in a temporal series, to whom there is such a thing as before and after, then and now; He ceases to be the eternal God. In other words, He becomes a finite

THE CHRISTIAN VIEW OF MAN

being; He becomes not God but *a god*, and even if we could become acquainted with him we should still have to search for the God who is God indeed.

It would be difficult to imagine a view that is more utterly unphilosophical than this view that God stepped voluntarily aside and was dependent for the rest of His plans upon what His creatures would deign to do. But it is just as unscriptural as it is unphilosophical. If one thing lies at the basis of the whole Biblical teaching about God it is that God knows all things. But He does not know all things if He does not know what His creatures will do. Such a God with limited knowledge is very different from the God of the Bible, the God before whom no secrets are hid.

Also very unsatisfactory, however, is the other form in which the theory with which we are dealing has been held. According to that other form of the theory, while God does not determine or foreordain the actions of the personal being whom He has created, but leaves their actions to the operation of their free will, yet He does know beforehand what their actions will be.

A little reflection, I think, will show that this form of the theory does not really overcome the difficulty that it was intended to overcome. The difficulty that it was intended to overcome was that if the actions of personal beings, including man, are to be free – if, in other words, they are to be really personal actions – they cannot be fixed beforehand. Therefore, the theory holds, they cannot have been fixed beforehand by God; therefore God must with respect to them have voluntarily limited the exercise of His power.

Well, but the trouble is that if God really created these personal beings, knowing beforehand what, if created, they would do, He did really determine their actions. Their actions were certain before they did them. But if the certainty of an action before it is accomplished means that the action is not a free or truly personal action, then those actions, being foreknown with absolute certainty by God, were not free; and the theory is open to all the objections that are urged against *our* doctrine.

It is open to all those objections. Yes, and it is faced by other objections of a much more serious kind.

What sort of God is it who merely knows beforehand that His creatures will perform certain actions and yet does not purpose that they shall perform those actions? Is it not a God who is aware of some necessity outside His own will? It does look as though that certainty of the future actions of those created persons which enables God to predict their actions must be due either to the purpose of God or to some blind fate, which God knows about but which is independent of God. The latter alternative dethrones God. Logically, it involves the abandonment of that high view which attributes the existence of all things to the mysterious will of an all-powerful person. It really involves the abandonment of a theistic view of the world, little though its advocates may be aware of such an implication.

No, we must discard all such compromises. They are exceedingly dangerous. But what settles the matter for us is that they are quite opposed to the Bible. The Bible makes no exceptions when it speaks of God's government of the world. According to the Bible, God governs all, and the Bible is particularly clear in teaching that He determines the voluntary acts of His creatures. Nothing, according to the Bible, lies outside of God's eternal plan.

But at that point a further objection is often raised. 'Are not you Calvinists forgetting one thing,' the objector says. 'If God foreordains even the free actions of the persons, including man, whom He has created, how about sinful

actions? Has He foreordained them? And if He has foreordained them, what becomes of His holiness? Must we
not attribute sinful actions, at least, solely to the free choice
of the sinners who commit them and not at all to the plan
or purpose of a holy God?'

In answer to the objection, it is easy to point to words of
Scripture which teach the exact opposite of the view that
the objector holds. The crucifixion of Jesus was certainly a
sinful act; no one can possibly have any doubt about that.
Yet the Bible says repeatedly that it was part of the plan of
God. 'Him, being delivered by the determinate counsel and
foreknowledge of God, ye have taken, and by wicked hands
have crucified and slain.'[1] The word here translated 'counsel' is a very plain word; it means 'wish' or 'purpose'. But
what was it that, according to this verse, was done thus by
the purpose of God? It was the delivering over of Christ.
I think that means the delivering over of Christ by Judas,
rather than the delivering over of Christ to His enemies by
God. If so, then the wicked act of Judas, his betrayal of
his Lord, is designated as something which was a part of
God's plan. But even if the delivering over that is meant
was the delivering over of Christ to His enemies by God,
we can hardly escape the plain implications of the passage.
It seems very clear, when the verse is taken as a whole, that
the entire crime by which Jesus was brought to His death
was accomplished, according to this verse, by the 'determinate counsel and foreknowledge of God'.

That is, if anything, even clearer in another passage in
the Book of Acts. In the fourth chapter of Acts it is said:
'For of a truth against thy holy child Jesus, whom thou hast
anointed, both Herod, and Pontius Pilate, with the Gentiles, and the people of Israel, were gathered together, for

[1] Acts 2:23.

to do what thy hand and thy counsel determined before to be done.'[1] Those wicked men, by their wicked act, were not defeating, or doing anything outside of, the plan of God. No, they did only what God's hand and God's counsel determined before to be done. Even the wicked acts of men are, therefore, no exceptions to the all-inclusiveness of God's eternal purpose. The Shorter Catechism is quite in accordance with the Bible when it says that by that eternal purpose God hath foreordained whatsoever comes to pass – not whatsoever comes to pass except the free or at least the wicked acts of created persons, but whatsoever comes to pass without any exception at all.

I remember a sermon that I heard last summer. I was at Zermatt in the Swiss Alps. On weekdays, I climbed the mountains; the Matterhorn, the Weisshorn and others of those great peaks. On Sundays I went to church.

The particular sermon that I now have in mind was one on the text: 'So let him curse, because the Lord hath said unto him, Curse David.'[2] Those words were spoken by David when he was fleeing from Absalom. As the king was passing along with his melancholy little company, Shimei cast stones at him and cursed him, and said: 'Come out, come out, thou bloody man, and thou man of Belial. The Lord hath returned upon thee all the blood of the house of Saul in whose stead thou hast reigned; and the Lord hath delivered the kingdom into the hand of Absalom thy son: and, behold, thou art taken in thy mischief, because thou art a bloody man.'[3]

Such was the cursing of Shimei. It is no wonder that Abishai the son of Zeruiah said unto the king: 'Why should this dead dog curse my lord the king? let me go over, I pray thee, and take off his head.'

[1] Acts 4:27 f.   [2] II Sam. 16:10.   [3] II Sam, 16:7 f.

But David said: 'What have I to do with you, ye sons of Zeruiah? so let him curse, because the Lord hath said unto him, Curse David. Who shall then say, Wherefore hast thou done so?'

The preacher in that little Protestant chapel in Catholic Switzerland took the incident as an example of the way in which God uses the actions of wicked men. David recognized a great truth. Even the cursing of Shimei, said David, had a place in God's plan. 'The Lord bade him curse me,' said David.

Of course, said the preacher at Zermatt, David did deserve cursing. He did not, indeed, at all deserve the particular cursing which Shimei heaped upon him: he was not a bloody man in his dealings with the house of Saul, as Shimei said he was. But for other things that he had done – for his murder of Uriah the Hittite, for his inordinate lust – he deserved cursing only too well.

There was One, however, said the preacher, of whom that could not possibly be said, and upon whom nevertheless curses were heaped. There was One who hung upon a shameful cross and endured the cursing and mocking of His enemies. They wagged their heads as they passed by and cursed and mocked him as He hung there upon the cross.

Those curses at least were entirely undeserved. They were directed against the one truly innocent man among all those who have ever lived upon this earth; they were black, horrible sin on the part of those who uttered them.

Yet they surely did not stand outside of God's plan. Nay, they were at the very heart of that plan. By those curses heaped upon the holy and just One, and by the death which went with them, we all, if we belong to God's people, are saved.

[42]

Yes, surely the wicked actions of men have a place in God's eternal purpose. The Bible makes that abundantly clear. Wicked men may not think they are serving God's purposes: but they are serving His purposes all the same, even by the most wicked of their acts.

At that point, however, serious questions might seem to arise. If wicked actions of wicked men have a place in God's plan, if they are foreordained of God, then is man responsible for them, and is not God the author of sin?

To each of these questions the Bible returns a very unequivocal answer. Yes, man is responsible for his wicked actions; and No, God is not the author of sin.

That man is responsible for his wicked actions is made so plain from the beginning of the Bible to the end that it is quite useless to cite individual proof texts. But it is equally clear in the Bible that God is not the author of sin. That is clear from the very nature of sin, as rebellion against God's holy law. It is also expressly taught. 'Let no man say when he is tempted, I am tempted of God,' says the Epistle of James: 'for God cannot be tempted with evil, neither tempteth he any man: But every man is tempted, when he is drawn away of his own lust, and enticed."

How, then, can we meet the difficulty? We have said that God has foreordained whatsoever comes to pass. The sinful actions of sinful men are things that come to pass. Yet we deny that God is the author of them and we put the responsibility for them upon man.

How can we possibly do that? Are we not involving ourselves in hopeless contradiction?

The answer is found in the fact that although God fore-

[1] James 1: 13 f.

ordains whatsoever comes to pass, He causes the bringing of those things to pass in widely different ways.

He does not cause the bringing to pass of the actions of personal beings in the same way as the way in which He causes the bringing to pass of events in the physical world. That is true even of the good actions of men who are His children. Even when God causes those men to do certain things by the gracious influence of His Holy Spirit, He does not deal with them as with sticks or stones, but He deals with them as with men. He does not cause them to do those things against their will, but He determines their will, and their freedom as persons is fully preserved when they perform those acts. The acts remain their acts, even though they are led to do them by the Spirit of God.

When God causes the bringing to pass of the *evil* actions of men, He does that in still a different way. He does not tempt the men to sin; He does not influence them to sin. But He causes the bringing to pass of those deeds by the free and responsible choices of personal beings. He has created those beings with the awful gift of freedom of choice. The things that they do in exercise of that gift are their acts. They do not, indeed, surprise God by the doing of them; their doing of them is part of His eternal plan: yet in the doing of them they, and not the holy God, are responsible.

What is the real difficulty here? Is it the difficulty of harmonizing the free will of the creature with the certainty of the creature's actions as part of God's eternal purpose? No, I do not think that that is the real difficulty. The real difficulty is the difficulty of seeing how a good and all-powerful God ever could have allowed sin to enter into the world that He had created. That difficulty faces not only the consistent and truly Biblical view of the divine decree which we have tried to summarize this afternoon, but it also faces the inconsistent views that we have rejected. It can never be used, therefore, as an argument in favour of any one of those inconsistent views and against the consistent view.

For both, the problem remains. How could a holy God, if He is all-powerful, have permitted the existence of sin?

What shall we do with the problem? I am afraid we shall have to do with it something that is not very pleasing to our pride; I am afraid we shall just have to say that it is insoluble.

Is it so surprising that there are some things that we do not know? God has told us much. He has told us much even about sin. He has told us how at infinite cost, by the gift of His Son, He has provided a way of escape from it. Yes, God has told us much. Is it surprising that He has not told us all? I do not think so, my friends. After all, we are but finite creatures. Is it surprising that there are some mysteries which God in His infinite goodness and wisdom has hidden from our eyes? Is it surprising that there are some things in His counsels about which He has bidden us be content not to know but instead just to trust Him who knows all?

4: What is Predestination?

IN THE LAST TALK I MAY BE CHARGED WITH HAVING spent all my time talking about one word – one word in the definition of the decrees of God that is found in the Shorter Catechism. It was only one word, but it was a tremendous word that might well have occupied all our Sunday afternoons for many years. 'The decrees of God,' says the Shorter Catechism, 'are his eternal purpose, according to the counsel of his will, whereby, for his own glory, he hath foreordained whatsoever comes to pass.' The word that I was talking to you about was the word 'whatsoever'. Has God foreordained *whatsoever* comes to pass, or has He foreordained only some of the things that come to pass, leaving other things – the things due to the choices of personal beings – outside of His eternal plan? I defended the former view, showing how that view alone is in accordance with the Bible. I maintained, in accordance with the Bible, that not some things that happen but all things – all things including the free choices of personal beings, all things including even the wicked actions of wicked men and devils – are brought to pass in accordance with God's eternal purpose.

Those things are not all brought to pass by God in the same way. God does not bring to pass the actions of personal beings in the same way as the way in which He brings to pass events in the physical world. He brings the actions of personal beings to pass in a way that preserves to the full their freedom of choice, and that does not at all destroy their responsibility. He brings to pass the wicked actions of personal beings in a way that does not at all make Him the author of sin. But that should not obscure in the slightest the fact that God does bring all things to pass. They are brought to pass in execution of God's purpose.

Wicked men may not think that they are serving God's purpose, but they *are* serving His purpose all the same, even by the wickedest of their acts. The crucifixion of Jesus Christ our Lord, the most terrible sin that has ever been committed upon this earth, was accomplished, according to the Bible, 'by the determinate counsel and foreknowledge of God'. Nothing whatever surprises God; all things that happen are absolutely certain from all eternity because they are all embraced in God's eternal plan.

People sometimes call that fatalism. It would be more correct to say that it is the diametrical opposite of fatalism. The difference between it and fatalism is the difference between fate and God, and surely there could be no greater difference than that. Fatalism grounds the certainty of all things in a blind, impersonal something that it calls fate; the view that we have presented grounds the certainty of all things in the holy purpose of a living God.

But the difference concerns far more than the ultimate grounding of all things. It would be utterly incorrect to say that we agree with the fatalist in holding that human freedom is a delusion and mechanism rules all, and differ from him merely in holding that back of the mechanism there lies the purpose of a personal God. Oh, no! We differ from the fatalist in a far more comprehensive way than that. We hold that just because the God that stands back of all things is a personal God, therefore there is a wonderful discrimination in the way in which He executes His decrees. We hold that when He deals with persons He deals with them as with persons, and that the certainty with which through them He accomplishes what He has purposed does not destroy their freedom or their responsibility but preserves it to the full.

In the presence of that certainty with which God accomplishes His purpose, we stand, indeed, in awe. 'It is a fearful thing,' says the Bible, 'to fall into the hands of the living God.'[1] Yes, it is a fearful thing indeed. But it is a very different thing from being in the clutches of a blind and impersonal fate. Biblical theism and fatalism are really at opposite poles.

Moreover, if the view that we have presented is the diametrical opposite of fatalism, it is also the only really formidable opponent of fatalism. Patchwork theologies, crazy-quilt views of the world that regard God's plan as being broken in upon here and there by the incalculable actions of personal beings, are not formidable opponents of fatalism at all. They bear too plainly upon their surface the marks of being nothing but compromises and makeshifts.

I suppose that is what a certain eminent scientist meant if he really did say, as he was once reported to me to have said, that from the point of view of science, Calvinism is 'the only respectable theology.' Calvinism alone does justice to the unity of the world, as it certainly alone does justice to the teaching of the Bible.

If, then, we hold to that high Biblical view, if we hold that whatsoever comes to pass comes to pass in accordance with the eternal purpose of God, can we know anything at all about what that eternal purpose is?

Yes, we can certainly know something about it. We cannot know all about it; what we know about it is very small compared with what we do not know: but still we do know

[1] Heb. 10:31.

something about it, and that something is very important indeed.

We do not know that something about it because we have discovered it by any searching of our own, but we know it because God has been graciously pleased to reveal it to us in His Word.

What then do we know about the purpose of God? Why did God create the universe? Why did He order it just thus and so?

Did He create and order the universe because of some purpose found in the universe itself? Surely not that. That would make the world an end in itself; it would elevate it to a position that belongs only to God. No, the creation of the world must have had as its purpose something that existed before the world was. But God Himself is all that existed before the world was. Therefore the purpose of the world must be found in God.

So we might reason, and if we so reasoned I think our reasoning would be good reasoning; it would be based upon what God has truly revealed to us regarding Himself. But we are not compelled to rely only upon such reasoning, good though the reasoning is. God has also directly told us what His purpose is. He has told us in the Bible that all things are brought to pass by Him for His own glory.

That truth is so pervasive in the Bible that I do not know whether I need to cite individual passages. I might cite such a glorious passage, for example, as the first chapter of Ephesians. There we are given as comprehensive an insight, perhaps, into the counsels of God as in any other one passage in the Bible. We are carried through the whole sweep of the divine plan beginning with God's choice of His people before the foundation of the world. But if that is where the majestic drama begins, where does it end? Does it end merely with the blessedness of the redeemed people; does it end merely with any blessedness of God's creatures? No indeed! Such blessedness is glorious. But it is not the end of all. There is something higher still, something to which that blessedness of God's creatures is merely a means. Why are the creatures blessed? The passage makes that perfectly plain. 'That we should be to the praise of his glory.' That is the ultimate end. The ultimate end of all things that come to pass, including the ultimate end of the great drama of redemption, is found in the glory of the eternal God.

Again and again that comes out in the Bible. The Bible differs from human books on religion not merely in this point or that but in the centre about which everything moves. Human books are prone to find that centre in man; the Bible finds it in God.

Men do not like that fundamental characteristic of the Bible. They prefer to think of the happiness of the creature as the goal; they wrongly interpret the text 'God is love' to mean that God is only love and that God exists for the benefit of His creatures; reversing the Shorter Catechism, they hold that God's chief end is to glorify man. But the Bible plainly agrees with the Shorter Catechism; the Bible plainly teaches that man's chief end – and the chief end of all things – is to glorify God.

People have a sort of vague notion that that attributes selfishness to God. It would be selfish and abominable for one of us to make his own glory the goal of his activities, and people jump to the conclusion that what is selfish in us is also selfish in God. So they try to find some goal of God's activities outside of God Himself.

Such reasoning, however, ignores the infinite gulf between the Creator and the creature. God is infinitely exalted above all finite creatures. If He made finite creatures the supreme end of His working, that would be to put a lower end in the place that belongs only to the higher. There is nothing higher than the glory of God. That therefore must be the supreme end of all things.

But what do we mean by the glory of God? I think it is very important for us to be clear about the answer to that question. We do not mean anything that is like the glory of a man. No, we mean something that is infinitely comprehensive. In the glory of God is comprehended the whole majesty of the divine perfections – infinite wisdom, infinite power, infinite goodness, infinite love. That it is – that full splendour of the being of God and the working of it, and the recognition of it in ceaseless praise – that it is which is the supreme end of all things. There can be no higher end; the substitution of any other end for it would be an abomination.

We hold, therefore, with all our souls to the great definition of the decrees of God in the Shorter Catechism of our Church. 'The decrees of God are His eternal purpose, according to the counsel of his will, whereby for his own glory he hath foreordained whatsoever comes to pass.'

We have treated in general the great truth set forth in that definition. It now remains to touch upon one particular sphere in which the truth is to be applied. I refer to the sphere of salvation. The doctrine of the divine decrees, when it is applied especially in that sphere of salvation, is called 'predestination'.

As I utter that word, some of my hearers may experience a shiver. 'Predestination' is thought to be such a very thorny doctrine; at least it is thought to be an idiosyncrasy of one particularly straight sect. It is often thought even by those who profess belief in it to be a doctrine which is better left aside in ordinary preaching – something to be relegated to the theological classrooms, but not something which will ever be acceptable to the rank and file of the Church.

Such is the way in which men are prone to look upon the matter. But just take up your Bible, my friends, and read it without prejudice. If you do so, you will be obliged to confess that the Bible looks upon the matter in an entirely different way. Far from relegating the doctrine of predestination to some secondary place, the Bible puts it right at the heart of all its teaching.

What then is the doctrine of predestination? Before I answer that question very briefly, I want to refer you to one or two things on the subject which I think, if you are interested, it would be useful to you to read.

In the first place, there is a splendid article by one of the very greatest of modern theologians, B. B. Warfield. It is entitled 'Predestination', and it is found in Hastings' *Dictionary of the Bible* and also in Dr Warfield's collected works, in the volume called *Biblical Doctrines*.[1]

In the second place, there is a popular treatment of the subject by Loraine Boettner, in a book called *The Reformed Doctrine of Predestination*,[2] which appeared just a few years ago and has been received in such a way as to show that interest in these great things of God's Word has by no means died out even in our unbelieving age.

Today I have time only to say a very few words about this great doctrine. I hope to come back to it; but just now I shall be able only to indicate briefly what the doctrine is, as the Bible sets it forth.

[1] This article appears in *Biblical Foundations*, published by Tyndale Press, London, in 1958.

[2] 12th printing, published by Presbyterian & Reformed Publishing Co., Philadelphia, Pa., in 1965.

I think I can make clear to you what the doctrine of pre-destination is by putting it in connection with what I have been saying in the last two talks.

I have been speaking of the eternal purpose of God, whereby for His own glory He has foreordained whatsoever comes to pass. Well, among the things that come to pass, according to the Bible, are the salvation of some men and the loss of others. If all things are foreordained by God's eternal purpose, then those two things are fore-ordained by it. The setting forth of the fact that they are foreordained by it is called the doctrine of predestination. That doctrine is just one particularly important applica-tion, therefore, of the doctrine of the divine decrees.

If that doctrine of the divine decrees is true, then this special application of it is true. That is clear.

But the Bible does not leave us to any such mere logic as that, good and inescapable though the logic is. It does not just let us get the doctrine of predestination by a mere inference from the general doctrine of the universality of the divine decree. No, it expressly teaches that doctrine of predestination and teaches it in the clearest possible way. The Bible clearly teaches that when some men are saved and others are lost, neither of these two things comes as a surprise to God, but both come to pass because they both stand in God's eternal plan.

The Bible lays the chief stress upon the former of these two things; it lays more stress upon the fact that the saved are predestined to their salvation than it does upon the fact that the lost are predestinated to their eternal retribu-tion.

Why does it do that? Does it do it because it seeks to obscure in any way the predestination of the lost? Cer-tainly not. On the contrary, it teaches that latter doctrine in certain passages in the clearest possible way. Why then does it lay the chief stress upon the predestination of the saved to salvation?

I think I can tell you at least one reason why it does so. It does so because it regards the salvation of the saved and not the eternal loss of the unsaved as the really surprising thing. *We* are prone to look at the matter in exactly the opposite way. The thing that *we* regard as surprising is that any members of the human race, any of those excellent creatures known as men, who are supposed to be doing the best they can and be guilty, at the most, of merely trifling and thoroughly forgivable faults, should ever fall under the divine displeasure. But the thing that the Bible regards as surprising is that any of those fallen creatures known as men, all of whom without exception deserve God's wrath and curse, should be received into eternal life. We regard it as surprising that any are lost: the Bible regards it as surprising that any are saved. Naturally it is the surprising or unexpected thing upon which the chief stress is laid. It is for that reason, or at least partly for that reason, that the Biblical doctrine of predestination is concerned chiefly with the predestination of the saved to their salvation rather than with the predestination of the unsaved to their eternal loss. The latter side of the matter is less extensively expounded simply because it is everywhere presupposed. It forms the dark background upon which the wonder of God's purpose for those whom He has chosen for salvation is thrown into glorious relief.

Why is it that some men are saved? Is it because of anything that they have done? Is it because they are less guilty in the sight of God than others? The whole Bible is concerned with denying that. God chose Israel, according to the Bible, from among all the peoples of the earth. Why?

Was it because Israel was more deserving of the divine favour, or because it possessed excellent qualities which God saw that He could use? A man who thinks so, a man who thinks that that is the meaning of the Old Testament, just shows thereby that he has never understood at all the heart of what the Old Testament teaches. Underlying everything else in the consciousness of the Old Testament people of God, as that consciousness was formed by the divine revelation given through lawgiver and prophets, was the profound sense of wonder that God had chosen such an insignificant people, a people not stronger or better than others, to be His peculiar people. Whatever else there may be in the Old Testament, that is the heart of it. But that is predestination. Israel was God's people, not because of anything that it had done or could do or might do, but simply because of God's sovereign choice.

When we come to the New Testament the same thing appears. There is in the New Testament clearer revelation of what the divine choice involves. New glories are revealed as being kept in store for the people of God. There is clearer revelation as to the persons who compose that people of God. It is a people chosen from among all the nations of the earth. But there is no change whatsoever in the basic revelation as to the sovereignty of the divine choice. According to the New Testament, as according to the Old Testament, those who form God's people, those who are destined to salvation, are chosen to form God's people, not because of anything that they have done or would do, but simply because of the sovereignty of God's good pleasure.

That sovereignty of God's good pleasure is the basic thing; everything else follows from it. Those whom God has chosen believe in Christ. But God did not choose them

[55]

because He foresaw that they would believe. It is exactly the other way around. They were not chosen by God because they believed : but they were enabled to believe because they were chosen by God. A man who misses that has missed something that lies very close to the heart of the Bible; he has missed the true meaning of the grace of God.

5: Does the Bible Teach Predestination?

IN THE LAST TALK I BEGAN TO SPEAK TO YOU ABOUT the great Scripture doctrine of predestination. That doctrine, I observed, is only one particular application of the doctrine of the divine decrees. If God foreordains by His eternal purpose all things that come to pass, and if among the things that come to pass are the salvation of some men and the loss of others, then it follows with inevitable logic that He foreordains both of these two things. God's foreordination of these two things has come to be called by the special term 'predestination'. The doctrine of predestination is just the doctrine of the divine decrees applied to the special sphere of salvation.

But the doctrine of predestination does not come to us merely as an inference from the general doctrine of the divine decrees; it is also expressly taught in the Bible in the clearest possible way.

Why is it, according to the Bible, that some men are saved and enter into eternal life, while other men receive the just punishment for their sin?

Is it simply because some men believe in Jesus Christ while others do not?

Well, certainly all those who believe in Jesus Christ are saved and all those who do not believe in Jesus Christ are lost. That is clear.

But why is it that some men believe in Jesus Christ, while others do not believe in Him?

Is it simply because some men, of their own free will, choose to believe in Christ, while others, equally of their own free will, choose not to believe? Is the human will thus the ultimate factor in this decision between believing and not believing?

Or do some men believe and others not believe, because they are foreordained to one or the other of these courses in the eternal purpose of God?

If the former alternative is right, the doctrine of pre-destination is wrong. If the human will is the ultimate factor in his choice between believing and not believing, between being saved and not being saved, then it is rather absurd to go on talking about predestination.

Some people do, indeed, indulge in that absurdity. Pre-destination, they say, means merely that those who believe are predestined to receive salvation. Whether they believe depends upon themselves, but once they have believed by their own choice, then they are predestinated to receive eternal life.

Surely that is a misuse of language. You can hardly speak of a thing as being 'predestined' – as being fixed be-forehand – if as a matter of fact it is not fixed at all but is uncertain until it is set in motion by an act of the human will.

The reason for such a misuse of language on the part of these people is plain. You see, they believe in the Bible. The Bible uses the word 'predestinate'; therefore they have to use that word, although they reject what that word, on any common-sense view of its meaning, would certainly seem to denote.

Let us not, however, lay the chief stress upon the word, but let us rather get back to the thing that underlies the word. Let us try just to get to the heart of the real question.

What is the real question at issue? I think I can tell you very plainly. It is the question whether a man is predestinated – if for the moment we concede to our adversaries in the debate their loose use of that term – it is the question whether a man is predestinated by God to salvation because he believes in Christ or is enabled to believe in Christ because he is predestinated.

That question is no mere unimportant or purely academic question. It is no mere theological subtlety. On the contrary, it is a matter of profound concern to the souls of men.

I know, indeed, that some truly Christian people decide the question wrongly; they are in error regarding this point and yet hold on to enough of the rest of what the Bible teaches in order that they may be really Christians. Yet it would be a great mistake to draw from that fact the conclusion that the question is unimportant. On the contrary, the more I have looked out upon the state of the Church at the present time, the more I have contemplated recent church history, the more firmly I am convinced that error regarding the question that we are now dealing with leads inevitably to more and more error, and often constitutes the entering wedge by which the entire Christian testimony of individuals and of churches is undermined.

Very well, if the question is so important, how shall it be decided? Shall it be decided merely by our likes and dislikes or by mere reasoning on our part as to what we would think right and proper? Shall one party to the debate merely say: 'I do not like this notion of an absolute predestination; I do not like this notion that the exact number and identity of the lost are fixed from all eternity in the purpose of God; I much prefer the notion that whether I am saved or lost depends on my own choice.' And shall the other party to the debate merely say, in reply to all that: 'I for my part like just the things that you do not like; I like the notion of an absolute predestination; I like to believe that when a man is saved that depends altogether upon God and not at all upon man; I prefer just to fall back, when I contemplate what is mysterious in this matter, upon the unsearchable counsel of God's will.'

Is that the way in which the debate shall be carried on? Shall it be carried on merely as a matter of likes and dislikes? I think not, my friends. Indeed, if it were to be carried on merely in that way, it would hardly need to be carried on at all. If this question is merely a question of our likes and dislikes, then it would seem to fall under the condemnation of the ancient adage that there should be no disputing about tastes. The whole dispute in that case had perhaps better stop. No, my friends. There is just one way to settle this question. It is to see what the Bible says about it. We shall never settle it by saying we like one answer better than another; but we shall settle it only if we listen to what God has said about it in His holy Word.

Very well, then; let us see what the Bible says about this matter of predestination.

But before we seek the Bible answer to the question, it is important for us to be perfectly clear about just what the question is.

We have already stated the question briefly. Are some men predestined by God to salvation because they believe in Christ, or are some men enabled to believe in Christ in the first place because they are predestinated? In other words, is predestination to salvation dependent upon that act of the human will known as faith, or is that act of the human will known as faith itself the result of predestination?

That is the question briefly put. But it is important to

observe that the former of the two answers to the question has been held in two different forms.

If predestination to salvation is held to be dependent upon a decision of the human will between faith and unbelief, then the further question arises whether God knows beforehand what that decision of the human will is going to be.

Some have said, 'No. God does not know beforehand what the decision of the human will is going to be; He simply waits to see what man will do, and then when man has finally acted God acts accordingly, bestowing salvation upon those who have chosen to believe and sending into eternal death those who have chosen not to believe.'

According to this view, the only predestination that we may speak of at all is a conditional predestination. It is predestination with a large 'if' attached to it. God does not predestinate any individuals to life or any others to eternal death but simply pre-establishes the general arrangement that *if* anyone believes in Christ he will enter into life and *if* anyone does not believe in Christ he will enter into eternal death. The decision as to which category any individual man will enter rests upon the individual man, and God does not even know how the decision will come out.

The other form in which the theory that we are dealing with is held attributes foreknowledge to God but not really foreordination. God knows beforehand, it holds, what the choice of any man will be as to believing or not believing in Christ, but He does not determine that choice.

This form of the theory, as we pointed out when we were dealing with the divine decrees in general, is a miserable hybrid. It is a half-way measure; it retains all the difficulties, real or supposed, which face the doctrine of a straight out-and-out foreordination by God of all things that come to pass, and it is also faced by overwhelming difficulties of its own.

But it is time to turn to the Bible. Fortunately the Bible is perfectly clear about this whole question. It is dead against both forms of the theory of which we have just spoken. It is utterly opposed to the view that God does not know what man will decide, and it is equally opposed to the view that what God foreknows He does not foreordain. Over against all such views, it tells us in the clearest possible way, not only in general that God has foreordained all things according to the counsel of His will but also in particular that He has foreordained the salvation of some men and the loss of others.

That appears really even in the Old Testament. Nothing could be more utterly abhorrent to the Old Testament revelation about God than this notion that the choices of man constitute a sort of exception to the sovereignty of God. If there is any one thing more than another about which the Old Testament is completely clear it is that God is absolute master of the heart of man. He can change the heart; He can take the old heart out and put a new heart in its place. These are just ways of saying that man's actions springing from man's heart do not lie outside the plan of God but form an integral part of it. God, according to the Old Testament, is King, and He is King with an absolute sovereignty which admits of no qualifications or exceptions whatsoever.

It is in exercise of that absolute sovereignty, according to the Bible, that God chose Israel. His choice of Israel was not due to any greatness or virtue which Israel could show. The Old Testament rings the changes upon that great thought. No, it was due to God's mysterious grace. Israel was God's people not because it had chosen to be

God's people but because it was predestinated to be God's people. A man who misses that has missed the heart and core of Old Testament revelation.

But when we come to the New Testament, what was really clear in the Old Testament becomes even more wonderfully clear and explicit. When men are saved, according to the New Testament, they are saved because of the mysterious foreordination of God.

I can only mention a few of the great passages in which that is taught.

It is taught in the teaching of our Lord reported in the Synoptic Gospels. When Jesus offered salvation, some accepted it and some turned away. Why? Simply because of the choice of men independent of the decree of God? Jesus Himself gives the answer. 'I thank thee, O Father, Lord of heaven and earth, because thou hast hid these things from the wise and prudent, and hast revealed them unto babes. Even so, Father: for so it seemed good in thy sight.'[1] 'It seemed good in thy sight' – there, according to Jesus, lies the ultimate reason why some received a saving knowledge of God and some did not.

It is taught with special clearness in the teaching of our Lord that is reported in the Gospel according to John. 'I pray not for the world,' says Jesus, 'but for them which thou hast given me.'[2] 'Thine they were,' says Jesus in a verse a little before, 'and thou gavest them me.'[3] I do not see how predestination could possibly be taught more clearly than it is in the whole of this high-priestly prayer of Jesus in the seventeenth chapter of John. A master thought – I think I might almost say *the* master thought in it – is that predestination precedes faith. The disciples belonged to God – that is in His eternal plan – before they believed;

[1] Matt. 11:25 f.   [2] John 17:9.   [3] John 17:6.

they did not come to belong to God because they believed, but they were enabled to believe because they already belonged to God and because in execution of His plan He drew them.

The same doctrine is taught in the Book of Acts. That is the book, be it remembered, that contains the famous answer to the question of the jailer at Philippi. 'What must I do to be saved?' said the jailer. 'Believe on the Lord Jesus Christ, and thou shalt be saved,' said Paul.[1] Salvation is here offered on the sole condition of faith in Jesus Christ. But how comes it, according to the Book of Acts, that some believe while others do not? The book gives the answer in the clearest possible way. Speaking of the preaching of Paul and Barnabas at Pisidian Antioch, it says that some of the Gentiles who heard them believed. Well, which of the Gentiles who heard them believed? Did those believe who simply chose of their own motion to believe? Not a bit of it! No, we are expressly told something entirely different. What does the book say about the matter? I will quote its exact words. 'As many as were ordained to eternal life believed.'[2] I do not see how it would be possible to put the doctrine of predestination more plainly or in fewer words than it is here put. Only those men believe in Christ who are foreordained thereto in the counsels of God. They are not predestinated because they believe, but they are enabled to believe because they are predestinated.

In the Epistles of Paul, the great doctrine of predestination is taught again and again and again. In fact, it would hardly be too much to say that it forms the basis of everything else that Paul teaches. The Apostle is concerned, moreover, to clear away any inconsistencies in the minds of his readers regarding this great doctrine; with an utterly

[1] Acts 16:30 f.   [2] Acts 13:48.

fearless logic he pursues our human pride into its last fast-
nesses and brings us face to face with the ultimate fact of
God's mysterious will.

'For the children being not yet born,' he says of Jacob
and Esau, 'neither having done anything good or bad, that
the purpose of God according to election might stand, not
of works, but of him that calleth, it was said unto her, The
elder shall serve the younger. Even as it is written, Jacob
I loved, but Esau I hated.'[1] How could it possibly be said
more plainly than in this passage that the predestination
of Jacob to salvation and of Esau to rejection was not due
to anything that they did or may have been foreseen as
doing – even to the foreseen faith of one and the foreseen
unbelief and disobedience of the other – but to the mysterious choice of God?

Then the Apostle takes up an objection. It is an objection that is still urged in the twentieth century against this
great doctrine of predestination. Does not the doctrine
attribute injustice or partiality to God?

Well, how does the Apostle deal with the objection?
Does he deal with it in the customary modern fashion of
receding from the position against which the objection
constitutes an attack? Does he explain away the doctrine
of predestination by saying that all he meant was a predestination conditional upon a man's future choices, or the
like?

Not at all! He does nothing of the kind; he does not re-
cede from his position a single inch; he does not explain
the doctrine away. On the contrary, he appeals again in
support of the doctrine to the sheer mystery of the sovereign will of God.

[1] Rom. 9: 11–13 (Revised Version).

'Is there unrighteousness with God?' – so the objection runs. 'God forbid,' says Paul in answer to it:

'For he said to Moses, I will have mercy on whom I will have mercy, and I will have compassion on whom I will have compassion. So then it is not of him that willeth, nor of him that runneth, but of God that sheweth mercy. For the scripture saith unto Pharaoh, Even for this same purpose have I raised thee up, that I might shew my power in thee, and that my name might be declared throughout all the earth. Therefore hath he mercy on whom he will have mercy, and whom he will he hardeneth. Thou wilt then say unto me, Why doth he yet find fault? For who hath resisted his will? Nay but, O man, who art thou that repliest against God? Shall the thing formed say to him that formed it, Why hast thou made me thus? Hath not the potter power over the clay, of the same lump to make one vessel unto honour, and another unto dishonour? What if God, willing to shew his wrath, and to make his power known, endured with much longsuffering the vessels of wrath fitted to destruction: and that he might make known the riches of his glory on the vessels of mercy, which he had afore prepared unto glory, even us, whom he hath called, not of the Jews only, but also of the Gentiles?'[1]

I do not see how the doctrine of predestination could be set forth more clearly than it is set forth here. But what is particularly to be observed is that this passage does not stand alone in the Epistles of Paul, and does not stand alone in the Bible. On the contrary, it only makes a little more explicit than usual what is everywhere presupposed.

[1] Rom. 9:14–24.

It really stands very close to the heart of what God has revealed to us in His Word.

All men deserving of God's wrath and curse, some men, and these not more deserving of God's favour than others, saved by His mysterious grace – these things are indeed at the heart of the Bible. Obscure them in the interests of human merit or human pride, and you have substituted man's wisdom for the Word of God.

In the next talk, I want to clear away certain misconceptions of the great doctrine of predestination. I want to say a few words to you about certain things that the doctrine of predestination does not mean. It does not mean that God's choice of some men for salvation is arbitrary or without good and sufficient reason – mysterious though the reason may be to us. It does not mean that God takes pleasure in the death of a sinner; it does not mean that the door of salvation is closed to anyone who will enter in; it does not mean that anyone in this life is reduced to the despair of knowing that God's grace will not be extended to him. Some of the horror with which this great doctrine of the Bible is often regarded is due to sad misconceptions regarding what it means.

But what I want to ask you to do just now is to take down your Bible and read what it says for yourselves. If you do that, I think you will be convinced that the doctrine of predestination, so distasteful to human pride, is really the only solid ground of hope for this world and for the next. Little hope have we, my friends, if our salvation depends upon ourselves; but the salvation of which the Bible speaks is rooted in the eternal counsel of God. There is no break and no possibility of break in the mighty working out of God's eternal plan. 'Whom he did predestinate,' says the Bible, 'them he also called: and whom he called, them he also justified: and whom he justified, them he also glorified.'[1] 'All things work together for good to them that love God' – how little comfort there would be in those words if the verse stopped there – if we had been told merely that all things work together for good to them that love God, and then we had been left to kindle that love of God in our cold dead hearts. But, thank God, the verse does *not* end there. The verse does not just say: 'All things work together for good to them that love God.' No, it says: 'All things work together for good to them that love God, to them who are the called according to His purpose.'[2] There, my friends, is the true ground of all our comfort – not in our love, not in our faith, not in anything that is in us, but in that mysterious and eternal counsel of God from which comes all faith, all love, all that we have and are and can be in this world and in the world to come.

[1] Rom. 8:30.   [2] Rom. 8:28.

6: Objections to Predestination

BEFORE WE PASS ON TO THE NEXT TOPIC IN THIS little series of talks, I think I ought to say just a few words more in explanation of the great Bible doctrine of predestination, about which I have been speaking in the last two talks.

That doctrine, we observed, applies the doctrine of the decrees of God to the special sphere of salvation. As God brings all things to pass by His eternal purpose in accordance with the counsel of His will, so He brings to pass thus in accordance with the counsel of His will the eternal salvation of some men and the just punishment of other men for their sins. Salvation, therefore, does not depend ultimately upon any act of the human will, even the act of faith in Jesus Christ. Faith itself is induced in those who are saved in accordance with the eternal purpose of God. They are not predestinated to salvation because they believe, but they are enabled to believe because they are predestinated.

We saw how very pervasive that doctrine is throughout the Bible. It is really taught by implication in the Old Testament, and it becomes fully explicit in the New Testament.

But clearly and fully though this great doctrine is taught in the Bible, a good many people – even a good many Christian people – have special difficulty with it.

Why have they such difficulty?

Well, partly, no doubt because the doctrine runs so directly counter to many of our preconceived ideas. It writes God entirely too large and man entirely too small to suit our human pride. We are so prone to make man's salvation depend on something that is in man.

Yet I think it would be a mistake to let our treatment of people's difficulties stop when we have said that. Some, even though not all, of the difficulties which people have with the doctrine of predestination are due to the fact that people do not understand the doctrine. They think the doctrine means what it does not mean, and so they turn aside from it with a horror which the true doctrine does not at all deserve.

I want therefore just now, in the present little talk, to tell you one or two things which the doctrine of predestination does *not* mean.

It does not mean, in the first place, that God's choice of some men for salvation while others are passed by is due to mere chance or that there is anything arbitrary about it.

We do not, indeed, know what the reason for God's choice is. We only know that whatever the reason for it may be, the reason is not to be found in any superior receptivity to the gospel on the part of those who are chosen; it is not to be found in any recognition by God of any superior capacity in them for faith in Jesus Christ. On the contrary those who are saved deserve eternal death just as much as do those who are lost, and they, exactly like those who are lost, are utterly unable to believe in Christ until they are born again by an act which is an act of God alone. Even their faith is worked in them by the Holy Spirit in accordance with God's choice of them from all eternity. Thus their salvation is not due to anything that is in them. It is a matter of pure grace.

But because *we* do not know what the reason is for God's choice of some and His passing by of others, that does not mean that there is no reason. As a matter of fact, there is without doubt an altogether good and sufficient reason. We can be perfectly sure of that. God never acts in arbitrary fashion; He acts always in accordance with infinite wisdom; all His acts are directed to infinitely high and worthy ends. We must just trust Him for that. We do not know why God has acted thus and not otherwise, but we know the One who knows and we rest in His infinite justice and goodness and wisdom.

I think the Christian man glories in his ignorance of God's counsels at this point. He rejoices that he does not know. The hymns of the evangelical church are full of celebrations of the *wonder* of God's grace. It is such a strange, such an utterly mysterious thing that God should extend His mercy to such sinners as we are. We deserved nothing but His wrath and curse. It would have been completely just if we had been lost as others are lost; it is a supreme wonder that we are saved. We cannot see why it is; we could not possibly believe it unless it were written so plainly in God's Word. We can only rest in it as a supreme mystery of grace.

In the second place, the doctrine of predestination does not mean that God rejoices in the death of a sinner. The Bible distinctly says the contrary. Hear that great verse in the thirty-third chapter of Ezekiel: 'As I live, saith the Lord God, I have no pleasure in the death of the wicked; but that the wicked turn from his way and live.'[1]

It may be the same thing that is taught in the First Epistle to Timothy, where it is said: God 'will have all men to be saved, and to come unto the knowledge of the truth.'[2]

This latter verse cannot possibly mean that God has determined by an act of His will that all men should be

[1] Ezek. 33:11.   [2] I Tim. 2:4.

[71]

saved. As a matter of fact not all men are saved. The Bible makes that abundantly clear; without that all its solemn warnings become a mockery. But if, when as a matter of fact not all men are saved, God had determined that all men should be saved, then that would mean that God's decree has been defeated and His will overthrown. In that case God would simply cease to be God.

The verse must mean something quite different from that blasphemous thing. That is clear. But what does it mean? I am inclined to think it means very much what that great Ezekiel passage means; I am inclined to think it means simply that God takes pleasure in the salvation of sinners and that He does not take pleasure in the punishment of the unsaved.

Another view has, indeed, been held by some. It has been suggested that the phrase 'all men' in this verse in I Timothy means 'all sorts of men,' and that the verse is directed against those who limited salvation to the Jews as distinguished from the Gentiles or to the wise as distinguished from the unwise. There is perhaps something to be said for such a view because of the context in which the verse occurs. But I am rather inclined to think that the phrase 'all men' is to be taken more strictly, and that the verse means that God takes pleasure in the salvation of the saved, and does not take pleasure in the punishment of those who are lost, so that so far as His pleasure in the thing directly accomplished is concerned He wishes that all men shall be saved.

At any rate, that is clearly the meaning of the Ezekiel passage, whatever may be true of the I Timothy passage; and a very precious truth it is indeed. The punishment of sinners – their just punishment for their sins – does, as we have seen, have a place in the plan of God.

But the Bible makes perfectly plain that God does not take pleasure in it for its own sake. It is necessary for high and worthy ends, mysterious though those ends are to us; it has its place in God's plan. But in itself it is not a thing in which He delights. He is good. He delights not in the death of the wicked but in the salvation of those who are saved by His grace.

In the third place, the doctrine of predestination does not mean that men are saved against their will or that they are condemned to eternal punishment when they want to believe in Christ and be saved.

I think that it is through this misconception that the really central objection to the great doctrine with which we have been dealing arises in the minds of so many people.

They have a sort of notion that the doctrine of predestination means that some people, before they decide whether to believe in Christ or not, can know beforehand whether they are predestined to salvation or predestined to destruction.

They imagine someone saying – on the assumption that the doctrine of predestination is true—'I have listened to the gospel; it touches my heart a little; I might possibly accept it: but what is the use? Whether I shall be saved or lost is all fixed beforehand anyway; what difference, therefore, does it make what I decide?'

Or – what seems even more horrible – they imagine someone saying, again on the assumption that the doctrine of predestination is true: 'I have listened to the gospel; I wish I were one of those who could accept it: but, you see, they are predestinated to salvation, they are among the elect of God; while I have been predestinated to destruction, so that, struggle as I may, there is for me no hope.'

Or – to take another example – they imagine someone saying, again on the assumption that the doctrine of predestination is true: 'I am among the elect of God; I can look down upon those who are not among the elect; and since I am among the elect I can live as I please, being assured that ultimately the plan of God for me will be worked out and I shall enter into eternal blessedness when I die.'

All three of these horrible examples, and many others similar to them, are based upon a totally wrong notion of what the doctrine of predestination means.

That doctrine does not mean that those who are predestinated to eternal life are saved against their will. On the contrary, only those who willingly embrace Jesus Christ as He is offered to us in the gospel are saved. Suppose a man says, 'I have decided not to have faith in Christ.' Can such a man comfort himself with the thought that perhaps he is predestinated to eternal life after all? Certainly not, provided that decision not to have faith in Jesus Christ is the man's final decision. No man who does not willingly have faith in Jesus Christ is saved. That is perfectly clear.

But when a man does willingly put his trust in Jesus Christ, does that act of the man's will lie outside the purpose of God? That is what the Bible most emphatically denies. No, it does not lie outside the purpose of God. No man is saved against his will. That is clear. But his will itself is determined in accordance with God's eternal plan.

I think I can make clear exactly what I mean if I take a very simple example from the Bible itself.

When Paul was in that ship of Alexandria being taken as a prisoner to Rome, he said to the frightened sailors and passengers: 'There shall be no loss of any man's life among you, but of the ship.'[1] He said that as a prophet, having received, as he expressly told the company, super-natural guidance. He had had revealed to him part of God's eternal plan. It was predestined in the purpose of God that no one on that ship was to lose his life. The preservation of every one of that ship's company was absolutely certain before it was accomplished.

Very well, then. So far so good. But what do we read a little farther down? What did Paul say to that ship's company a little later? Here is what he said: 'Except these abide in the ship, ye cannot be saved.' The sailors, namely, had been about to flee from the ship in the boat. To stop them Paul said to the centurion and to the soldiers: 'Except these abide in the ship, ye cannot be saved.'

He had previously told the ship's company that they would all be preserved alive. That came on the authority of God; it was absolutely certain; it was predestinated. Yet now he tells them that that thing which was absolutely certain to take place would not take place unless a certain condition were fulfilled. It would not take place unless the sailors stayed in the ship.

Did the laying down of that condition at all destroy the certainty of the working out of God's plan in accordance wih the previous prophecy? Not a bit of it! Why not? Simply because God provided for the fulfilling of the condition when He provided for the accomplishment of the final result for which the fulfilling of the condition was necessary.

Yes, it was certainly true that the ship's company would not be saved unless the sailors remained in the ship. But that did not involve any risk that the plan of God might be

[1] Acts 27:22.

defeated. You see, the sailors did remain in the ship, and so the original prophecy went straight on to its fulfilment.

Those sailors did not remain in the ship by chance. No, they were, although they did not know it, under the guiding hand of God. The centurion and the soldiers who kept them in the ship were God's instruments in seeing to the final accomplishment of God's plan.

We learn by this simple example a very great truth. It is simply this – that when the final result is foreordained by God all the steps to it are also foreordained. Straight through all the apparently tangled course of human history runs the accomplishment of God's eternal plan.

Apply that to the matter of faith and salvation, and I think some of your difficulty with the doctrine of predestination will disappear. God has predestinated some men to final salvation, just as He predestinated to the preservation of their earthly lives those men who were on the ship. Yet in both cases the fulfilment of a condition was necessary to the accomplishment of the final result. The men on that ship were all predestinated to get safely ashore; yet they would not have finally got safely ashore unless the centurion had kept those sailors in the ship. So God's elect are all predestinated to eternal salvation; yet they will not attain eternal salvation unless they believe in the Lord Jesus Christ.

Does the interposition of a necessary condition introduce any uncertainty in the final accomplishment of God's plan? Not a bit of it! Not in either case. Not in the simple case of the preservation of that ship's company on that ship of Alexandria, and not in the case of the salvation of God's elect. In both cases God has provided for the fulfilment of all the conditions just as truly as He has provided for the accomplishment of the ultimate end.

But is our sense of the freedom of our will at all incompatible with the complete certainty of God's ordering of our lives? Well, I am just going to appeal at this point to any man within the sound of my voice who is aware of the moment when he was born again. Not all Christians are aware of the moment when they were born again. All have been born again, but not all know when they were born again. But some can give the very moment when they were saved. I am appealing now to any one of these.

You were born again at that blessed moment, were you not, my brother? Now was that your act or God's act? The Bible tells you it was God's act – 'which were born, not of blood, nor of the will of the flesh, nor of the will of man, but of God.' And your experience confirms the Bible, does it not? You know in your inmost soul that it was God's act. You were blind and God made you to see. God did it, not you. You are as sure of that as you are sure of anything in this world.

Now at the moment when you were born again you believed in Christ. That was the immediate sign of your being born again, and it was due solely to the wonderful regenerating power of the Spirit of God. Well, my brother, did that wonderful act of God do violence to your freedom as a person? Did you feel that the new-found faith that you had in the Lord Jesus Christ was any the less your act – a free choice of your will – because it was due to the resistless regenerating act of the Spirit of God? I think not, my friend. I think rather that you will be inclined to say you never were so free as you were at that blessed moment when in absolutely resistless fashion the Holy Spirit of God worked faith in you and you turned to the Lord Jesus Christ as your Saviour and Lord.

No, indeed, the eternal plan of God and even the execution of that plan at the supernatural act of regeneration or the new birth are not in the slightest degree incompatible with our freedom and our responsibility as personal beings.

What a great mistake it is, then, to think that the doctrine of predestination is contrary to the free offer of salvation to all. Of course that offer is given to all. Of course it remains true in the fullest and richest sense that whosoever will may come. None who will trust in Christ is excluded. None, I say, none without any exception whatsoever.

Never have we any right to assume that any man or group of men that we can name is outside of God's plan for salvation; never have we any right to assume that any man upon this earth is beyond the reach of the grace of God; never have we the right to withhold the gospel from any man wherever he may be.

But when we thus proclaim the gospel, what a comfort the doctrine of predestination is! What a comfort it is to know that salvation depends solely upon God's mysterious grace! We all deserved to perish in our sins, and so did all those to whom we preach. But God's grace is wonderful. He has in His eternal plan a people chosen for His name. Happy are we if we are God's instruments in gathering into His kingdom any of those who from all eternity belong to Him.

7: God's Works of Creation and Providence

HAVING SPOKEN OF THE DECREES OF GOD, I COME now to speak of the way in which God executes His decrees.

But is God's execution of His decrees to be distinguished from His decrees themselves? There have, I believe, been those who have said, 'No'. With God, they say, to plan is the same thing as to act; finite creatures, they say, may plan first and act afterwards, but God's plan and God's action are the same thing. Indeed, some of those who engage in this way of thinking go, I believe, still further. With God, they say, not only is action the same as purpose, but purpose is the same as thought. We, they say, can think a thing and not do it, but for God to think a thing is to purpose that it shall come into being, and for Him to purpose that it shall come into being is the same as to bring it into being. The vastness of the universe, they say, is simply the unfolding of the thoughts of God. But these persons are mistaken; they have fallen into a very serious error.

It is certainly true that to God there is no eternal obstacle to the making realities of all of His thoughts. He has infinite power, and anything that He thinks, He can do.

But because everything that He thinks, He can do, it does not follow that everything that He thinks, He does do. The things that He does actually do are chosen with perfect wisdom out of an infinity of things that He chooses not to do. Never ought we to confuse God's thoughts with His purposes.

Indeed, if we did fall into that confusion we should be

in danger of obscuring the true nature of the personality of God. If God purposes everything that He thinks, if there is no selection in His purposes among the things that He contemplates, then it might almost be said that the purposes of God are only falsely called purposes and become rather the involuntary unfolding of some impersonal dialectic process.

But if God's purposes must be distinguished from His thoughts, a further distinction must also be made. As God's purposes must be distinguished from His thoughts, so also His actions must be distinguished from His purposes. There is a true distinction between the decrees of God and the execution of His decrees.

To obliterate that distinction is again to engage in a perversion of a truth.

It is perfectly true that everything that God purposes comes inevitably to accomplishment. *We* purpose many things that we do not bring to pass, but it is not so with God. What He purposes He always does.

It is perfectly true also that there is no before and after to God. He is beyond time; He is infinite and eternal; He does not have to wait, as we do, for any stream of time, independent of Him, to bear Him on to the point where He can engage in the execution of His several decrees. All things to Him are eternally present. It might seem, therefore, as though in His case there were no interval and indeed no distinction between a decree and the execution of the decree, no distinction between purpose and act.

Such reasoning, however, is fallacious and dangerous. Even if we cannot apply temporal notions to the life of God, even if therefore there is to Him no interval, in the ordinary sense, between purpose and act, still there is an important distinction between the two. It is still important to remember not only that God is all-wise in His plans, but also that He is all-powerful in His acts.

But is it true to say even that there is no interval of time between God's purposes and His actions, between His decrees and the carrying out of His decrees? I think it is but a half-truth.

It is true that God, being eternal, is beyond time. But that is not to say that time has no real existence; it is not to say that time as we know it is a mere semblance. No, what we ought to say, as I think I heard one of my teachers say years ago, is that God created time when He created finite things. He *really* created time, and we really stand in a temporal sequence. Therefore we are not uttering an untruth when we say that He purposed long ago what He brings to pass now. All things that come to pass were in His purpose from all eternity, but He brings them severally to pass at those points in the order of time which He in His infinite wisdom has fixed. We who stand, as finite creatures, in the order of time observe the gradual unfolding of the execution of God's eternal plan; and as we observe its gradual unfolding, as we observe the way in which, without haste yet with perfect sureness, God's purposes are worked out, we join in praise of Him to whom a thousand years are but as yesterday when it is past and as a watch in the night, in praise of Him whose ways are not as our ways and whose thoughts are not as our thoughts, who in infinite wisdom has planned all things from the beginning and brings all things to pass according to His eternal purpose and in His own good time. Thus do all finite creatures and the very order of time in which they stand serve the eternal purpose for which they were created, which purpose is the glory of God.

Holding therefore that there is a true distinction between

God's decrees and the execution of His decrees, we are prepared to ask how God executes His decrees. The Shorter Catechism says, in answer to that question: 'God executeth His decrees in the works of creation and providence.'

I want to say a few words in turn about God's work of creation and God's works of providence.

With regard to the work of creation, the Shorter Catechism says that is God's making all things of nothing.

I think we ought to pause a few moments to ask what that means.

The answer is in the main surely not difficult. Look out upon the vast universe in which we are living. How did it come into being? Various answers have been given, but the answer of the Bible is plain. The universe came into being, the Bible says, by the act of a personal God; it came into being because God made it. That has at least the merit of being easy to understand.

But what is meant by the words 'of nothing' in that definition? What is meant when it is said that God made all things 'of nothing'? Two things at least are meant.

In the first place, it is meant that God did not make all things of something; He did not make the universe out of some already existing material.

A great many people have held that when God made the universe He found some material ready to His hand. He moulded that material, they say; He gave it its form; He reduced it from chaos to order: but the material was already there.

Then the question arises: 'Whence came that already existing material?'

When we look at the world as it is, we ask naturally how it came into being. We can trace its processes back a certain distance. Everything, we say, has a cause. This thing happened because that thing previously happened; and that thing in turn happened because some still earlier thing happened. So we can reason from effect to cause through a prolonged series. But unless the series is really infinite, we come at length to the beginning of the series. All the causes that we see in the world about us were in turn caused by other causes; but at the beginning of the series must stand a First Cause, a cause that is not caused by anything else.

What is that First Cause? The simple Christian, with his Bible open before him, has a ready answer. The First Cause is God. The universe came into being, he says, by the voluntary act of an infinite and eternal Person.

That answer has the merit of simplicity. There is something wonderfully satisfying about it. It does not make the mistake that so many philosophies do of giving to what is lower an honour that would seem rightfully to belong to what is higher.

I do make bold to say that when a man has once had the veil taken from his eyes, so that he can think of God as the personal God, the living God, the sole and all-sufficient First Cause of all things, he wonders at his former blindness and pities with all his soul those who still do not understand.

How sadly this simple answer to the riddle of the universe is marred or rather destroyed by those who say that when God made the universe He made it out of something! If God made the universe out of something, then that something was already in existence, and in existence independently of God, when the universe was made.

In that case, what do we arrive at when we start out in our search for a First Cause, what do we arrive at when we

[83]

trace back the things that now are to their causes, and then those causes back to still earlier causes of which they in turn are effects, until we get to a cause which was not produced by any previous cause, which in other words was the First Cause? Why, on the theory about which we are now speaking we get to not one First Cause but two First Causes – God and the material which He used when He made the world. But two First Causes are one too many. A doctrine like that will never be a satisfactory view of the world. It gives us a blind inert material which is quite unfitted to be regarded as a First Cause, and it gives us a God who is no God at all. It gives us a God who is not really infinite but is limited in His working by a world-stuff which does not owe its being to Him.

From such dualism – if you will pardon me for using a somewhat technical word – we turn with relief to the high theism of the Bible. Our God, the God of the Bible, is no mere artificer, using as best He may the material put into His hands, but He is the great originator of all things that are. There are not two First Causes – God and the material that God used – but one First Cause, God and God alone.

That is the first thing that we mean when we say that God made all things of nothing. We mean that He did not make all things of something; we mean that He did not make all things out of some previously existing material.

But there is another thing that we mean when we say that God made all things of nothing. We mean that He did not make all things of the substance of His own being.

If He made all things out of the substance of His own being, then all things are a part of God, and we have an error akin to the deadly error of pantheism.

There are many who have fallen into that error. The world, they hold, is an emanation in the life of God; it is an unfolding of His being; its stuff is the stuff of which He Himself is composed.

That error, like so many other errors of which we have spoken, is the perversion of a great truth. It is certainly true that the universe proceeded from God as its cause. When the Bible teaches us that all things were made of nothing, that does not mean that all things came into being without a cause. On the contrary, all things came into being with a thoroughly adequate cause – namely, God.

It is perfectly true, moreover, that when God brought the universe into being He did not do so without reference to His own nature. On the contrary, He acted in accordance with His own infinite wisdom. The creation of the world was not an arbitrary act, but it served high and worthy ends, and those ends were in accordance with the Creator's infinite goodness and wisdom.

But, in saying all that, we are not at all saying that the universe proceeded by some process of emanation from the being of God. On the contrary, it was created by an act of God's will. God did not owe it to anyone to create the world, and the creation of the world was not necessary to the completion of His own life. God is absolutely self-sufficient; He was fully God before the world ever was created, and the present existence of the world is not necessary to His divine life. 'Before the mountains were brought forth, or ever thou hadst formed the earth and the world, even from everlasting to everlasting, thou art God.'[1] Being God from all eternity, He determined for His own high and worthy ends to bring this universe into being. We can only stand in awe before the Creator's infinite wisdom and power.

Thus it is highly important for us to stress those words

[1] Ps. 90:2.

[85]

'of nothing', in that definition of the Shorter Catechism. God did not make all things of something already existing, and He did not draw forth all things out of the substance of His being; but He made all things of nothing.

But if those words 'of nothing' are to be stressed in that definition, we should also not forget the words 'all things'. We should not forget the fact that in God's work of creation, 'things' were created.

There have been many who have denied that. There is no such thing, they say, as an external world. When I contemplate a tree, they say, all I really have knowledge of is the idea of the tree in my own mind. I cannot really go beyond what is in my mind. But are there other minds? I have never been able to see that people of this way of thinking really have any right to hold that there are. A consistent idealist, I am inclined to think, ought to hold that even other minds have no existence except as an idea in his own mind. But consistently or not, many idealists do hold that there are other minds, and many of them hold that there is a supreme mind, and that the universe exists only in that supreme mind, the mind of God.

Against such a philosophy, the Christian, with his Bible open before him, ought to believe in the existence of an external world. I think he ought to quote with approval what I remember hearing Dr Warfield quote years ago: 'What is mind? No matter. What is matter? Never mind.' Mind and matter ought not to be confused. And certainly the Christian ought to hold that our minds and the matter of which our bodies are composed, and this whole universe to which our bodies and our minds belong were truly created by an act of the all-wise and all-powerful God.

What sort of universe is this which thus came into being

by the act of the all-powerful God? Is it a good universe or is it a bad universe? Pessimists have said that it is a bad universe. Indeed, some of them have said that it is the worst universe that could possibly have been created. What does the Christian say?

The Bible gives the answer very simply, in words of one syllable: 'And God saw every thing that he had made, and, behold, it was very good.'[1] No, this universe is not a bad universe. Nothing that God makes is a failure. It is not a bad universe but a good universe.

Indeed, it is the very best universe that could possibly have been created. God is never content with the second best; there are no limitations either to His wisdom or to His power; nothing that He does varies by a hair's breadth from that which is absolutely best.

When we say that the universe is the best that could possibly have been created, we do not, of course, mean that it is the best for our ends, and we do not necessarily mean that it is the universe that conduces the most to our pleasure. On the contrary we are obliged, sooner or later, to learn the hard lesson that the universe was not made for our enjoyment alone. We have to learn to take the universe as it is.

Accepting the universe is the root idea of a book by a brilliant and thoughtful sceptic of the present day – Walter Lippmann's *Preface to Morals*, which was a 'best seller' a few years ago. A baby, says Walter Lippmann, thinks that the universe is run just for its peculiar benefit; all that it has to do is to reach out its little hand and those things will be given to it that satisfy its wants. But then as it grows older it learns that very often the reached-out hand has to be drawn back empty; it learns that there is a vast world

[1] Gen. 1:31.

outside quite indifferent to its desires. When it really learns that, it is becoming mature.

Many men, says Walter Lippmann, never do become thoroughly mature, never do really grow up, never do really get rid of the notion that the universe either is or ought to be run for their benefit. In order to get rid of that notion, says he, it is not sufficient that a man should have mere knowledge of details about the universe. A boy can take you out into the night and rehearse to you a great many facts about the stars, but unless he 'feels the vast indifference of the universe to his own fate, and has placed himself in the perspective of cold and illimitable space, he has not looked maturely at the heavens.'

Well, we can go with Walter Lippmann part way. We can go with him in what he says on the negative side. We can go with him in holding that the universe does not exist for our particular benefit, and that we are worse than petulant children if we complain because of that fact.

Only, we differ from him profoundly in what he seeks to substitute for this petulance of babyhood. He seeks to substitute for it what he calls 'disinterestedness' – the recognition of and acquiescence in the fact that the universe is indifferent to our fate. We substitute for it the conviction that the universe was created for the glory of God.

For that end, the glory of God, though not for the ends that we might have cherished, this universe is the best universe that could possibly have been created. To that end those starry heavens of which Walter Lippmann speaks contribute their part. When we contemplate their vastness we are impressed indeed with our own insignificance. We can go with Walter Lippmann so far. But unlike Mr Lippmann we do not stop there. To us the stars have no merely negative message; they do not merely tell us what we are not. But they also tell us what God is:

> 'The spacious firmament on high,
> With all the blue ethereal sky,
> And spangled heavens, a shining frame,
> Their great Original proclaim.'

Or, in the words of holy Scripture, of which that hymn of Joseph Addison is after all but a feeble exposition, 'the heavens declare the glory of God, and the firmament sheweth his handywork.'[1] The end for which the universe was made is not indeed our enjoyment. But that does not mean that we know nothing about what the end is. The end, the Bible tells us, is the glory of God. And that end the universe attains in God's own way.

But are those starry heavens, is that vast fabric of nature, really indifferent to our fate? The Bible has something to say about that also. 'And we know that all things work together for good to them that love God, to them who are the called according to his purpose.'[2] But those who can take to themselves the comfort of that text are not those who regard themselves, in childish fashion, as the end for which the creation exists; but they are those who have been enabled to find their true blessedness, and the true purpose of all the world, in singing the Creator's praise.

[1] Ps. 19:1.   [2] Rom. 8:28.

8: God's Works of Providence

IN THE LAST TALK I SPOKE TO YOU ABOUT GOD'S work of creation. It is a mysterious subject, yet the teaching of the Bible about it is, in its great outlines, plain. How did this vast universe come into being? The answer of the Bible is very simple. God made it. He did not make it out of some already existing material, and He did not draw it from His own being; but He made it of nothing. By His act of creation, that came to be which before was not.

When God had thus created the universe, what was His relation to the universe that He had created? No relation at all, said the deists of one hundred and fifty years ago. The universe, they said, was allowed by its creator to run of itself like a vast machine, and it is vain to seek any interference or governance from the great artificer.

That deistic view is now out of date. I do not think that it is widely held today – at least among educated people. But other errors, equally serious, have taken its place.

Some have said that there is no such thing as a continued existence of the universe at all, but that God creates it anew every instant. All God's governance of the world is thus regarded as a work of creation; the work of creation is regarded as the only work in which God executes His decrees.

That view at first sight might seem to do honour to God. It denies to the world any continuity of existence, and finds in the creative activity of God the only continuity that there is. But in point of fact that view does not really do honour to God but endangers very seriously our sense of the distinction between God and the world. If the world has no continuous existence, then it is hard to see exactly how God can be regarded as distinct from the world. But the distinction between God and the world that He has created is at the heart of what the Bible teaches us about God.

There are other ways also in which this theory of continuous creation can be shown to be contrary to God's Word. The Bible plainly teaches the real existence of the world; the continuity of the universe is not, according to the Bible, a mere semblance. When God created the universe He created a true order of nature operating under laws established for it by its creator. The Bible distinguishes sharply God's creation of the universe from God's government of the universe already created.

The truth lies, then, neither with those who say that the universe once created continued thereafter to exist without any activity of God, nor on the other hand with those who say that all the continuity which the world seems to possess is simply the continuity of a constantly repeated act of creation. Where then does the truth lie?

The truth lies in the Biblical doctrine of providence. That doctrine is summed up in the following answer of the Shorter Catechism:

'God's works of providence are, his most holy, wise, and powerful preserving and governing all his creatures, and all their actions.'

Notice in the first place that in this definition God is said to *preserve* all His creatures. What does that mean? It means that according to the Bible nothing in the whole universe would continue to exist for one slightest fraction of a second without God. We have said that the universe has real existence; its continuity is not a mere semblance.

[91]

But that does not mean that it exists independently of a continued activity of God. On the contrary it would cease to exist the very moment God should withdraw His preserving hand.

In the second place, the Shorter Catechism says that God's works of providence are His *governing* of all His creatures and all their actions. God's activity in the universe that He has made is not limited to His keeping it from destruction. He also works in it and through it in positive fashion, bringing to pass through it those things that are in accordance with His eternal plan.

We noticed that fact when we were dealing with the decrees of God. All things that happen in the whole universe are included, we observed, in God's purpose; nothing that happens surprises God. But now we are speaking of the ways in which God accomplishes His purpose, the ways in which He carries out His plan. One of those ways in which He accomplishes His purpose is to be found in His works of providence.

When God accomplishes His purpose by His works of providence, is it God that works or is it the forces and the persons created by Him?

Some have said that it is only the forces and the persons created by Him. The people who have said that are the deists, of whom we have already spoken. They hold that the activity of God in the universe is limited to the initial work of creation, and that, once created, the universe runs itself like a machine, without interference from God. It is perfectly clear that that deistic view is quite contrary to the Bible.

Others have said that it is God only that works, and that the forces and persons created by God do not really work at all. Everything that happens, they say, is an immediate work of God. God, they say, is the only cause, and it is only in appearance that within the course of the world one thing can be said to cause another.

Thus, according to this view, when we see a bullet hole in a pane of glass and ask what caused it and come to the conclusion that it was due to the firing of a gun across the street, we have no real right to talk in any such way; we have no real right to say that the hole in the glass was caused by the passage of the bullet through the glass, and the passage of the bullet through the glass was caused by the firing of the gun, and the firing of the gun was caused by the pulling of the trigger, and the pulling of the trigger was caused by the action of the man who had the gun in his hand. Not at all, say the persons of the way of thinking with which we are now dealing; this whole idea of cause within the course of this world is merely an illusion. What we call cause is really only observed sequence. The making of the hole in the pane of glass came after the firing of the gun, but we cannot say that it was caused by it; the emergence of the bullet from the gun came after the explosion of the powder in the cartridge, but we cannot say that it was caused by it. No, what we commonly think of as a relationship of cause and effect between different things in the course of the world, they say, is really only the observed manner of God's working. God, they say, is the only cause.

Is such a way of looking at the matter correct? Where can we get the answer to that question?

Well, we cannot get the answer from the scientists. They have usually no help to give us at this point. It is their business, they tell us, to observe what happens, not to explain how it comes to happen. They are content – at least many of them are – to leave the whole question as to what is meant when we say that one thing causes another to the philosophers and theologians.

Now I am expressing no opinion as to whether this modesty on the part of the scientists is wise or unwise. Possibly it may turn out that it is unwise. Possibly it may turn out that in being indifferent to the question whether the so-called forces of nature have real existence or are a mere semblance the scientists have deprived science of its true dignity and its true basis, and that in the long run science even in detail may feel the ill effects of such degradation. Possibly, in other words, it may be important for science, as for every other branch of human endeavour, to be based upon a sound philosophy. No doubt it is better for the scientists to refrain from any philosophical opinion whatever than to do what they have so often done – namely, dish out to us a very crude philosophy as though that crude philosophy itself were science. But the best thing of all would be for them to have a true philosophy. It is better to have no philosophy at all than a bad philosophy, but it would be still better to have a good philosophy.

However that may be, whatever the effects in the field of what in the narrow sense of the word is called science, it is quite clear that to hold that God is the only cause and that nothing in the universe can be said to be the cause of anything else is quite disastrous to the moral life of man, and quite disastrous to man's view of God.

This opinion involves logically the complete denial of human responsibility. If the firing of that gun across the street is not the cause of the passage of the bullet through the pane, then the man who fired the gun cannot be said to be responsible for what damage the bullet may have done or for the death of anyone whom it may have killed.

This view involves also a real denial of the holiness of God. If God alone acts and the forces apparently operating in the world are merely ways of His working and are not really themselves working at all, then what we call the universe is merely a phase of the life of God, and the distinction between God and the world is broken down. But that distinction between God and the world is quite fundamental in any high view of God. It involves what the Bible calls the holiness of God. To break it down is disastrous indeed.

The Bible gives no warrant whatever for any such view, but plainly teaches that there are forces truly operating in the world. The theologians speak of those forces truly operating in the world as 'second causes'. God is the First Cause, but the forces of nature and the free actions of personal beings whom God has created are second causes; and it is extremely important, if we would be true to the Bible, that the existence of second causes should not be denied.

Thus when it is asked whether, when anything happens in the course of nature, it is some force of nature or God that causes that event, the true answer is, 'Both'. That event is caused by a force operating in the world and it is caused by God.

Only, it is very important to observe that the two causes are not on the same plane. They are not coordinate, but one is completely subordinate to the other. In every event in the natural world God has completely accomplished what He willed to accomplish. He is not limited in any way by the forces of nature or by the free actions of His creatures. They truly act; but they truly act only as He has determined that they shall act. The correct way, therefore, of expressing the relationship between second causes and God, the great First Cause, is to say that God makes use of second causes to accomplish what is in accordance with His eternal purpose. Second causes are not independent forces whose coöperation He needs, but they are means that He employs exactly as He will.

That is what the Shorter Catechism means when it says that 'God's works of providence are, his most holy, wise, and powerful preserving *and governing* all his creatures, and all their actions.'

Stress should be laid also upon that word 'all'. No actions of created things lie outside the field of God's works of providence. By them all He brings to pass what He has determined in His eternal plan.

How pervasive is God's government of the world! It includes, in the first place, the ordinary operations of nature – rain, snow, hail, sunshine, the sprouting of the seed, the ripening of the grain. With what matchless beauty is this part of God's care for His creatures set forth in the One Hundred and Fourth Psalm:

'He sendeth the springs into the valleys, which run among the hills.

They give drink to every beast of the field: the wild asses quench their thirst.

By them shall the fowls of the heaven have their habitation, which sing among the branches.

He watereth the hills from his chambers: the earth is satisfied with the fruit of thy works.

He causeth the grass to grow for the cattle, and herb for the service of man: that he may bring forth food out of the earth;

And wine that maketh glad the heart of man, and oil to make his face to shine, and bread which strengtheneth man's heart.

The trees of the Lord are full of sap; the cedars of
   Lebanon, which he hath planted;
Where the birds make their nests: as for the stork, the fir
   trees are her house.
The high hills are a refuge for the wild goats; and the rocks
   for the conies.
He appointed the moon for seasons: the sun knoweth his
   going down.
Thou makest darkness, and it is night: wherein all the
   beasts of the forest do creep forth.
The young lions roar after their prey, and seek their meat
   from God.
The sun ariseth, they gather themselves together, and lay
   them down in their dens.
Man goeth forth unto his work and to his labour until the
   evening.
O Lord, how manifold are thy works! in wisdom hast thou
   made them all: the earth is full of thy riches.
So is this great and wide sea, wherein are things creeping
   innumerable, both small and great beasts.
There go the ships: there is that leviathan, whom thou
   hast made to play therein.
These wait all upon thee; that thou mayest give them their
   meat in due season.
That thou givest them they gather: thou openest thine
   hand, they are filled with good.
Thou hidest thy face, they are troubled: thou takest away
   their breath, they die, and return to their dust.
Thou sendest forth thy spirit, they are created: and thou
   renewest the face of the earth.'

Have we outgrown that wonderful passage? Have we outgrown the conviction that God feeds the lions that roar

after their prey in the night, that He provides a habitation for the birds of heaven, that all His creatures, small and great, wait upon Him that He may give them their meat in due season? Have we outgrown the words of the Lord Jesus when He said that God has so clothed the lilies of the field as that even Solomon in all his glory was not arrayed like one of these? Have we outgrown His conviction that not a sparrow falls to the ground without God, and that God feedeth them from day to day?

Has scientific agriculture or the scientific study of botany or biology made these things to be out of date? Have we with our overmuch knowledge outgrown that simple conviction of Jesus and of the Psalmist that every living creature receives its meat from God?

Well, my friends, if that is so, if these things have really come to be out of date, then we have lost far more than we have gained. We have gained knowledge in some directions, but we have lost a knowledge that is vastly more important than all the knowledge that we have acquired.

Let us not blame science for that loss. There is nothing in modern science that invalidates the teaching of the Bible regarding God's care for His creatures; nay, there is much that wonderfully confirms it, if only we had eyes to see. Something quite other than true science has put the mist and darkness over men's eyes.

When will the lost simplicity and the lost profundity be regained? Only when God in His supernatural grace shall have removed the blindness of sin in order that again men may see. When that blessed day comes, men will look out again upon the wonders of the world with the profound simplicity of the Psalmist, and will detect in all the processes of nature no mere cold unguided working of some mechanical force but the mysterious and infinitely discriminating hand of the living God.

Are, then, God's works of providence limited to His use of the impersonal forces of nature? Is there a little island of resistance to His will here in the midst of His world – a little island of resistance in the form of the free actions of personal beings? Are those actions beyond His governance? Has He, so far as they are concerned, abdicated the throne of His power?

We saw in dealing with the decrees of God that there are some who say, Yes. But we saw also that the Bible says, No. The Bible plainly teaches that God works His will just as surely through the free actions of personal beings including man as He does through the courses of the heavenly bodies or the silent ripening of the grain.

I need not now repeat the proof of that fact. It is writ large in the Bible from Genesis to Revelation. God, according to the Bible, is master of the heart of man just as much as He is master of the impersonal forces of nature, and from man's heart man's actions come.

Even the wicked actions of men serve God's purposes and it is by His works of providence that He permits those wicked actions to be done.

Just pass in review, my friends, the history of Bible times. Nation after nation rises on the scene – Egypt, Assyria, Babylon, Persia, Rome. Wicked nations are these – cruel, hard and proud. Yet how does the Bible represent them? How does the Bible represent even the cruel devastations that they carried on amid the people of God? As defeating God's eternal purpose, as contravening His governance of the world? No, my friends, the Bible represents those wicked nations as unwitting instruments in God's almighty hand.

Take also the wicked acts not of nations but of individual men. Were *they* accomplished without the providence of God; did *they* defeat His governance of the world? The Bible tells us, No. 'Ye thought' – said Joseph to his wicked brethren – 'Ye thought evil against me; but God meant it unto good, to bring to pass, as it is this day, to save much people alive.'[1] Even the supreme crime of all the ages, the crucifixion of Jesus our Lord, was not brought about apart from the providence of God. 'For of a truth,' says the Book of Acts, 'against thy holy child Jesus, whom thou hast anointed, both Herod, and Pontius Pilate, with the Gentiles, and the people of Israel, were gathered together, for to do whatsoever thy hand and thy counsel determined before to be done.'[2]

No, my friends, there are no exceptions here. Everything that is done in the whole course of the world – by forces of nature or by the free actions of men good and bad – everything has God as its great First Cause.

But though God brings all these things to pass, He brings them to pass in widely different ways. He does not bring to pass the free actions of personal beings in the same way as the way in which He brings to pass the ripening of the grain. He brings to pass the actions of personal beings in a way that preserves their freedom and their responsibility to the full.

Shall that be accounted a thing inconceivable? We persuade our fellow men, yet their freedom is preserved when they do what we persuade them to do. Shall not then God be able to do with certainty what we with our little power do with uncertainty? Does not God who made the soul of man know how to move it in accordance with its own nature so that its freedom shall not be destroyed?

[1] Gen. 50:20.   [2] Acts 4:27 f.

Shall He not be able even to use the evil actions of men for His own holy purposes? The Bible tells us plainly that He does so use those evil actions. Even they do not lie beyond His governance as the great First Cause. Yet the Bible tells us with equal plainness that He is not the author of sin but that sin is ever hateful in His eyes. Why He allowed sin to enter is the mystery of mysteries, but that He did so we are plainly told, and that He did so for some high and holy end.

Thus all nature, including the nature of man, is a wondrous instrument of many strings, delicately tuned to work God's will and upon which He plays with master hand. But all such figures of speech go only a little way; there is a point at which they break down. The relationship of God to the course of nature is vastly more intimate than the relationship of a musician to the instrument upon which he plays. The musician is outside of his instrument as the engineer is outside of the machine that he controls and guides. But God pervades the course of nature. No recess of it is apart from Him; He pervades it through and through. Infinitely separate, yet everywhere near – such is the great mystery of the immanence and transcendence of God.

And is that all? Does God, now that the course of nature has been made, operate only in and through that course of nature? Or does He operate and has He operated in a way that is above nature? Are His works of providence now His only works, or does He work – or has He at any time worked – in such creative fashion amid the course of the world as He did when He first called the world into being from the abyss of nothingness by His initial creative word?

With that question – the question of the supernatural – we shall deal in the next of these talks.

[101]

9: Miracles

IN THE LAST TWO TALKS I SPOKE TO YOU, FIRST, about God's work of creation, and, second, about God's works of providence. The distinction between the two is important, because upon it depends our belief in the real existence of the world. If God's work of preserving and governing the universe is the same thing as His work of creating the universe, if creation has to go on constantly every instant, then it follows with inevitable logic that the thing created at any one instant does not remain in existence.

Such a view is quite contrary, we observed, to the Bible. The Bible plainly teaches the real existence of the created universe.

God created the universe by His work of creation; and then He preserves and governs the created universe by His works of providence.

But did God's work of creation take place all in one act at the very beginning, so that after that initial act all God's works in the universe are works of providence and none of them are works of creation? When God had once created the world, did He thereafter work only through the course of nature that He had made? Or did He also from time to time act directly, without the use of means, as when He first called the world into being by His creative fiat?

I can see no reason whatever why we should assume, before investigation, that the former of these alternatives must be correct. I can see nothing antecedently improbable in the second alternative. Why should it be thought incredible that God who once created the world out of nothing should again put forth His creative power? Why should it be thought incredible that He who once acted without the use of means should again choose so to act? Why should it be thought necessary that God, when once He had created the course of nature, should ever thereafter limit Himself to the use of that course of nature and should never act in a way that is above nature and independent of it?

Those questions, I think, are unanswerable. There is no reason whatever why anyone who really believes in creation should regard as impossible an entrance into the world already created of God's creative power. What God has done once, He obviously can do again. He acted independently of the course of nature when He created the course of nature in the first place. He may, therefore, act in equal independence of the course of nature at any time when He will.

Such an act of God, independent of the course of nature, would properly be called 'supernatural'. It would not be contrary to nature; for one of God's actions is never contrary to another: but it would certainly be 'above nature'. The possibility of supernatural acts of God, entering into the course of nature, cannot be denied by anyone who really believes in God's initial act of creation.

But if supernatural acts of God, entering into the course of the world, are perfectly possible, are they also actual? God might conceivably perform them, but has He actually done so?

That question can be answered only by an examination of the record of God's actions which is found in the Bible. And when the record is examined, the answer that it gives is found to be perfectly clear. The Bible plainly records the

THE CHRISTIAN VIEW OF MAN

occurrence of acts of God which are not natural but supernatural.

Those supernatural acts of God, those supernatural
events recorded in the Bible, are of two kinds. Some of
them are in the external world. These are events witnessed
by the bodily eye or at least events which might conceivably be witnessed by the bodily eye. Others of them are
events within the hidden realm of the soul.

I cannot think that this distinction goes to the very
depths of things. We must guard ourselves against thinking
that a supernatural event in the soul of man is less supernatural than a supernatural event in the external world.
On the contrary, we ought to think of it as just as supernatural and just as wonderful. We must also guard ourselves against thinking that a supernatural event in the soul
of man is without effects in the external world. On the
contrary, it has very obvious effects in the external world.
When a supernatural change is wrought in a man's soul,
the man's actions become different. The effects of the
supernatural change in the man's soul are quite visible and
quite tangible. They appear to all observers; they are very
decidedly in the external world.

Nevertheless, the distinction about which we are speaking, though the importance of it ought not to be exagger-
ated, is still important. We ought not to ignore it. We ought
not to ignore the fact that the supernatural events recorded
in the Bible are of two classes. Some of those events are in
the external world and some of them are not.

Those that are in the former class, those that are events
in the external world, are properly called miracles.

The Bible contains a great many accounts of miracles,
both in the Old Testament and in the New Testament.
Among the New Testament miracles are, for example, the

feeding of the five thousand, the walking of our Lord upon the water, the raising of Lazarus from the dead, the resurrection of our Lord Himself.

But just what is a miracle? How is the word 'miracle' to be defined? The answer has already been given in what we have just said. 'A miracle is an event in the external world that is wrought by the immediate power of God.' I have never seen any reason to abandon that definition, which I learned from one of my teachers a great many years ago.

In saying that a miracle is an event that is wrought by the immediate power of God, we do not mean that while miracles are acts of God, other events are not acts of God. On the contrary ordinary events are just as much acts of God as miracles are. Only, in the case of ordinary events God uses means, He uses the order of nature that He has created in order to bring those events to pass; while in the case of miracles He uses no means but puts forth His creative power as He put it forth when He first made all things of nothing.

Various other definitions of miracles have been proposed. Thus it has sometimes been said that miracles are just extraordinary events of which we in our ignorance do not know the cause. They have some natural explanation, it is said, but we do not know what it is. If we ever do learn what the natural explanation of any of these events is, the event will cease to be to us a miracle. So, it is said, many events formerly regarded as miracles are now not regarded as miracles at all. The progress of science, it is said, has put them out of the miracle-category.

It is perfectly evident that that definition of miracle really destroys any true distinction between miracles and other events. The only distinction that remains according to that definition is found in our ignorance. A miracle is defined as an event about the cause of which we happen just now to be ignorant. Well, in that case it does not in itself differ from any other event. Such a definition really denies the distinctness of that which is being defined. Those who favour it really deny, by implication, that there are any events outside of the course of nature. All events, they hold, have a natural explanation, even though in the case of some events we do not happen to know what the natural explanation is.

Very similar is the definition, favoured by some rather devout people, to the effect that a miracle is an event brought about by the operation of some higher law of nature than the laws which we know. Take a miracle like the feeding of the five thousand, for example. It seems at first sight to be entirely incapable of explanation under the laws of nature. According to all the laws of nature that we know, five loaves and two small fishes could not have been multiplied suddenly so as to feed five thousand men. Well, then, are we to say that in bringing that event to pass God disregarded the laws of nature that He Himself had established? Not at all, say the advocates of the definition that we are now considering. God did not disregard His own laws. No, He merely used some law of nature higher than the laws which He has been pleased to reveal to us.

I have said that this definition of a miracle is similar to the definition that I considered a moment ago. I should have said that it is not only similar to that definition, but actually identical with it, except for the fact that the people who put the definition in this latter form often seek to preserve a certain special prerogative of God in the case of the events called miracles. I think they are usually inclined to say not only that we do not now know the laws that were operative in the events that we call miracles but that we never shall know them. They are mysterious laws which God has chosen to hide from us.

But even so this definition denies anything really distinctive in a miracle. Like every other event, a miracle according to this definition is an event that takes place in the course of nature and in accordance with nature's laws.

Why should a definition like that be advocated? Why do some people – even some rather devout people – seem to dread so much the simple admission that God has chosen from time to time to enter in creative fashion into the course of the world, not acting in accordance with the laws of nature that He has established but acting as He acted when He first made the world out of nothing by the word of His power?

Well, I think these people have a sort of notion that unless God acts always in accordance with the laws of nature that He has established He is introducing an element of disorder and arbitrariness into the course of the world. Would God break His own laws? they indignantly ask. If He did do so, would that not be a sort of confession that His own laws are imperfect or unrighteous? Would it not almost mean that God had broken faith with us? He has placed us here in this course of nature. He has led us to depend upon the regular operation of its laws; He has led us to have confidence that the sun will rise in the morning and set at night, that spring will follow winter and summer will follow spring. How can He then without something like bad faith enter arbitrarily into the orderly course of this universe that He has made? If He did so, would it not destroy the security that He led us to expect when He placed us here under a reign of natural law?

In answer to that objection, I just ask you to consider whether the mere fact that we are under a reign of natural law is the thing that gives us security. Is this universe such a very safe place to live in after all? There are some exceedingly destructive forces in nature; and man, who is himself part of nature, bids fair to use those forces for the destruction of the race. Every now and then we read something about lethal rays or wings over Europe or the like. These things are fiction, but there is a large measure of scientific basis for them. Great progress in bombing planes and poison gases undoubtedly was made during the World War. Without doubt far greater progress still has been made since the war was over. Scientists tell us that the atom, infinitesimal though it is, contains a boundless store of energy. Who can tell us when man may discover the secret of releasing that energy? And when man discovers the secret of releasing it, what possible security for any of us will be left?

There are astronomical possibilities of destruction also beyond number. Great stars are destroyed, and our earth is a mere speck of a satellite revolving around one of the smaller of the stars, which we call the sun. The destruction of such a tiny fragment would not cause very much of a jolt in the vast machinery of the universe.

There are, moreover, possibilities in the course of nature far more appalling than the sudden destruction of the whole human race and of the earth on which it lives. They are the possibilities that arise from man's tyranny over man. Before us today there rises with ever-increasing menace the spectre of a tyranny of the experts – a tyranny compared with which all the tyrannies of the past are as nothing – a tyranny which would bring the details of life under expert regulation and make mankind's dreams of freedom and glory to be a thing of the past. Such a tyranny has made great strides in Germany and Russia in our day.

It menaces us here in America. It menaces all men everywhere. If it gains control of the race, better would it have been by far that mankind should never have appeared upon the earth.

Sometimes I feel tempted to be appalled when I think of these things. I look out upon all that is sweet and beautiful in the world, and then think with what a very precarious tenure that is all held. If we consider what we know of nature and of that part of nature that is called man, we can almost say that the very existence of humanity hangs by a thread.

Where then is security to be found, if indeed it can be found at all? Well, I will tell you. It is not to be found in nature; least of all is it to be found in that part of nature that we call man. I will tell you where it can be found. It is to be found only in God.

What guarantee have I that someone will not invent a poison gas that will be capable of wiping out the population of whole cities by the dropping of a single bomb? What guarantee have I that the secret of atomic energy may not be discovered, to the destruction of the human race? What guarantee have I that all the high aspirations of humanity will not come to an utterly brutal and meaningless end?

I have no guarantee in nature; and I have no guarantee in man. There is nothing whatever in the composition of the universe, so far as we know it, to put these things outside the bounds of possibility.

How then do I retain my equanimity in view of the appalling possibilities revealed by modern science? How do I know that whatever may be the end of the human race upon this earth, it will not be a brutal and meaningless end, but will be an end that will accomplish some high and holy purpose?

In one way and in one way only – through my faith in God. There are destructive forces in nature. We may well be in terror if we think of those forces as being turned loose upon us. We shall be still more in terror if we think of those forces as getting into the control of scientific experts; for the tyranny of experts is the most soul-crushing tyranny that could possibly be set up.

There is one way and one way only to overcome such terror. It is to remember that all the destructive forces of nature, and even the scientific and pseudo-scientific experts that are such a menace to freedom, are instruments in the hands of an all-wise God. We can contemplate lethal rays and the boundless stores of dangerous energy said to be contained in the atom, and the menace of tyrannical power placed in the hands of 'psychiatrists' and other experts who often stand on very low moral ground, without losing all hope – we can contemplate such things for one reason and one reason only – because we have faith in God. Very terrible things may come upon the human race, but not the brutal and meaningless destruction which might seem to be so imminent today. We can trust God, you see, for that. God has His purposes; He has revealed something of them in the Bible; and we can trust Him to carry them out. Our trust is not in nature but it is in God.

But if our trust is in God, it does not make any essential difference how God chooses to bring His counsels to pass. He does so partly through the course of nature; He rules all things in nature by His providence. But if He chooses to do so in part in a way that is independent of nature, that does not in the slightest destroy our confidence in His wisdom and in His goodness and in His power.

Miracles, in other words, are not arbitrary events. They do not introduce the slightest disorder into the course of nature. They are indeed above nature, but they proceed from the source of all the order that nature contains – namely, from the all-wise and all-holy decree of the living God.

To some extent we can detect the reason for miracles. The miracles of the Bible are due – for the most part, let us say, to be very cautious – to the fact of sin. When God created the world it was all very good. But then sin was introduced. Why God permitted it we do not know. That is the mystery of mysteries. But that He did so for high and holy ends we are sure. Sin introduced a terrible rent into the course of nature. To heal that rent God put forth His creative power in the miracles of the Bible, especially the great miracles of the incarnation and the resurrection of Jesus Christ our Lord. Do those blessed miracles destroy our confidence in the regularity of nature's laws? Certainly not. But why not? The answer is plain. Simply because they are acts of the same God as the God to whom nature's laws are due. God does not contradict Himself.

Miracles today have ceased. I think there is some confusion on that point among Christian people. Have not some of us witnessed miracles, they say. A loved one has lain upon a bed of sickness. The physicians have given up the case; they have warned us that there is no hope. But then Christians have prayed; they have brought their dear one before God in prayer. God has graciously heard the prayer, and the loved one has been raised up. Is not that a miracle?

We answer, No. It is a very wonderful work of God, but it is not a miracle. When we prayed God for the recovery of that beloved person we were not asking God to work a miracle like the healing of blind Bartimaeus or the raising of Lazarus from the dead. No, we were just asking Him to use the resources of nature for the recovery of our loved one.

Often we ask a human physician to do that same thing. Someone is stricken down. If the physician is not called in promptly the person dies. But the physician is called in and the person lives. How does the physician attain that end? Well, not by a miracle, but by a skilful use of the remedies which nature affords.

But why should not God be asked to do what a mere finite person is asked to do? His power is vastly greater than that of the physician. Why may He not be asked to use those vast resources of nature, which He, unlike the human physician, holds in the hollow of His hand?

Or take this matter of praying for rain. Ought we to pray for rain? we are often asked. If we say, Yes, the modern sceptics hold up their hands in horror. Could such obscurantism, they say, possibly be imagined as surviving in the twentieth century? Rain and sunshine are governed, they say, by meteorological laws. Do you mean to tell us, they ask, that those laws can be set aside by your prayers?

Well, my friends, I cannot for the life of me see that to pray for rain involves asking God to set aside meteorological laws. It is not at all beyond the bounds of possibility that even man may learn to use those laws for the production of rain and sunshine as he wills. We hear about that possibility every now and then. If it becomes actuality, we may think of ourselves very soon as applying to Washington to the F.W.C.A. – Federal Weather Control Administration – asking them please to send us the kind of weather that we desire.

I hope for my part, indeed, that we shall never arrive

at that point. I hope – despite the droughts and sand-storms in the West – that we shall never learn how to control the weather; for if we do there will be very serious disputes as to the kind of weather that we shall have, so that what is now the only really safe topic of casual conversation may become a cause of civil war. But at least human control of the weather is not by any means outside the bounds of possibility. Why then may we not ask God to do what we might conceivably ask even man to do? Why may we not ask God to use the resources of nature in order to send gentle rain and refreshing streams? God governs the course of nature. It may well prove to be His will to use that course of nature and use even our humble prayers to send refreshment to a thirsty land.

There is one advantage in asking God for rain, as compared with asking some bureaucrat in Washington. We can be perfectly sure in the case of God, as we cannot be sure in the case of a bureaucrat in Washington, that He will not grant our request if to do so is unwise or would work injustice to someone else.

Such an ordering of the resources of nature by God is not a miracle; and I repeat what I have already said, that in our day miracles have ceased.

They have not ceased for ever; but for the present they have ceased. There is a good reason why they have ceased.[1] But though miracles have ceased, certain other supernatural acts of God are wrought every day, when men and women are born again by the mysterious creative work of the Holy Spirit that the Bible calls the new birth. We hope to have something to say about those supernatural acts of God before we have finished this little series of talks.

[1] See Warfield, *Counterfeit Miracles*, pp. 3-31.

10: Did God Create Man?

WE HAVE BEEN SPEAKING ABOUT THE WAYS IN which God works, the ways in which He executes His decrees. He executes His decrees, we observed, first, by His work of creation, and, second, by His works of providence.

Then, in the last talk, we discussed the question whether God's work of creation ceased altogether after His works of providence began. Did God perform His work of creation all in one act, and ever thereafter limit Himself in His working to a use of the order of nature that He had already created; or did He from time to time enter into the course of nature in supernatural fashion, not using means but acting immediately, by His creative power?

We saw that the latter answer is correct. The Bible contains a record not only of God's works of providence, but also of certain events which were produced by God without the use of means but by an immediate exercise of His power. Those events, when they took place in the external world, as distinguished from events like the new birth which take place in the hidden realm of the soul, are called miracles.

The miracles recorded in the Bible are – for the most part at least, if we may be very cautious – events that took place in connection with God's work of the saving of His people from sin. That is true, I think, of the miracles of the Old Testament as well as of the miracles of the New Testament. By certain miracles of the Old Testament God defended His chosen people and authenticated the true commission of His servants, the prophets. But the choice of one

[114]

people from among the peoples of the earth, and the necessity for sending the prophets with the particular message that they had were due to the entrance of sin into the world.

Then, however, the question arises whether there were not other supernatural acts of God, coming after God's first work of creation and yet so basic in the very constitution of the world as we know it that we think of them rather as acts of creation producing the course of nature than as miracles entering into a course of nature already produced.

In other words, did creation take place all at once, or did it take place in several successive acts of God?

I suppose the first impulse of most Christians, as they read the first chapter of Genesis, is to give the second answer to this question. The Book of Genesis seems to divide the work of creation into six successive steps or stages. It is certainly not necessary to think that the six days spoken of in that first chapter of the Bible are intended to be six days of twenty-four hours each. We may think of them rather as very long periods of time. But do they not at least mark six distinct acts or stages of creation, rather than merely six periods in which God moulded by works of providence an already created world?

It is not so easy to answer that question as might at first sight be supposed. Mr John Murray, who is in charge of the Department of Systematic Theology in Westminster Seminary, to whom I am indebted in a great many ways this autumn and last spring in my preparation for this little series of talks, has called my attention, for example, to an interesting article by B. B. Warfield – published now in his collected works – on 'Calvin's Doctrine of the Creation'.[1] In it Dr Warfield points out that John Calvin was

[1] B. B. Warfield, 'Calvin's Doctrine of the Creation', in *Calvin and Calvinism*, 1931, pp. 287-349.

THE CHRISTIAN VIEW OF MAN

inclined to reserve the term 'creation' to God's initial act
by which He made things strictly of nothing, and to avoid
using that word to designate the subsequent acts of God
mentioned in connection with the six days of the first chapter of Genesis. Those subsequent acts would thus appear
to have been regarded by Calvin as a moulding by God of
what He had already created rather than as additional acts
of creation in the strict sense.

I think we had better not stop to consider this somewhat
difficult question, but had better proceed at once to speak
of the origin of man.

At that point at least – that is, in connection with the
origin of man – Calvin, as Dr Warfield points out, found
a work of creation in the very strictest sense of the word;
and I think every careful reader of the Bible who accepts
the Biblical account as true must agree with him. The
origin of man, according to the Bible, was not due solely
to God's works of providence, to God's governing of the
course of nature that He had already created, but it was
due to an act of God that was truly supernatural. God did
not merely order the course of nature in such fashion that
man should be produced, but He created man.

When I say that, some of my hearers may turn away in
disgust. 'Do you mean to tell us,' they may say, 'that you
hold to that antiquated theory of special creation? Why,
everybody knows today that man was evolved from lower
animals; even an elementary study of the bodily structure
of man as compared with that of other animals shows that
beyond peradventure; the theory of evolution has established itself firmly, and a person who rejects it is an ig-
noramus who is not worth listening to for a moment.'

Well, before I am finally dismissed in this summary
fashion, I wonder whether I might just be permitted to say

a word or two with regard to the way in which this question seems to me to present itself. I do not feel in the slightest degree competent to discuss the question with any fulness. There are colleagues of mine in our Faculty to whom I should be obliged to refer you. But I do want to tell you very briefly what I think the question at bottom is.

The real question at issue here is the question whether at the origin of the race of mankind there was or was not a supernatural act of God.

We have seen that there is a really existing course of nature. The things that that course of nature brings forth have God, indeed, as their first cause, but they have secondary causes within the course of nature itself. They are brought forth by God, but they are brought forth by Him by a use of the course of nature that He has made.

We have also seen that from time to time God has entered into the course of nature in direct fashion, not using the course of nature already made, but acting in a way essentially similar to the way in which He acted when He first made all things of nothing by the word of His power.

When such supernatural acts of God are in the external world, as distinguished, for example, from the hidden realm of the soul, they are called, as we have seen, miracles.

Now the miracles of the Bible are often closely interwoven with events which are not miracles but natural events. So our Lord placed His fingers in a man's ears on one occasion when He healed the man of his deafness. Placing His fingers in that man's ears was certainly not a miracle. But in connection with that perfectly natural event a miracle was wrought. We do not know just exactly where the natural event ended and the miracle began; but we do know that a miracle was wrought. God did use natural means there; but the natural means were not sufficient to produce the result. There was also, in addition to the use of natural means, a miracle.

So it is also, according to the Bible, with the creation of man. There was a use of the course of nature already made. The Bible expresses that in simple language when it says that 'God formed man of the dust of the ground'. But there was also something more than the use of the course of nature already made. The Bible expresses that in various ways. It expresses it, for example, when it says that God created man in His own image. It seems clear that the word 'created' is there to be taken in its strictest and loftiest sense.

But is the Bible right when it says that? Is the Bible right in teaching that a supernatural act of God took place at the beginning of the life of the human race?

A great many people say, No. Modern science, they say, has shown clearly that man is the product of evolution.

Well, I ask how it has shown that. In reply to that question, I am told that the most minute similarity exists between the structure of man and the structure of the lower animals. The real state of the case is, then, that an unbroken line of generations unites man with other forms of animal life.

Now I am not going to argue at all about the facts to which appeal is made in this connection. I am not competent to do so, and fortunately I do not think that I am obliged to do so. The question that I am raising just now is concerned not so much with the facts as with the relevance of the facts to the real question at issue.

Let us see whether we can bring the question right out into the open, where we can look at it a little better.

At first sight it does not seem to be very much out in the open. It seems to be hidden away in a region of great mystery. The origin of the first man took place a long time ago. We do not know exactly when it took place; even the Bible does not really tell us that. We do not even know exactly where it took place. It seems, therefore, to be very remote from us. We are somewhat confused by our sense of that remoteness.

Very well, then, let us take something that lies a good deal nearer at hand. The origin of the first man, which believers in the Bible declare to be a supernatural event, lies very far off; but the origin of the human life of another man, which believers in the Bible declare to be also a supernatural event, lies in the full light of historical times and in a country that is perfectly well known.

If you go down to a steamship ticket office today you can buy a ticket to a little country called Palestine, which lies on the eastern shore of the Mediterranean Sea. The history of that country is fairly well known. There have been obscure periods in its history – for example, during parts of the Middle Ages – but there was one period in its history about which we have rather abundant information. That was the highly literate and civilized period during which Palestine was under the Roman Empire.

In order to learn something of the men and the animals that lived in that period, you do not have to draw inferences from any scanty fossil remains; you do not have to learn of the succession of events from the way in which the strata in the earth's crust are superimposed one upon another.

No, we have glorious sculptures coming from that period and still more glorious ones coming from a slightly earlier period in Greece. We have moreover historical records, and many kinds of vivid descriptions of the kind of life men lived in that age. In Egypt there have even been discovered a great many private letters which people wrote to one another in those days. From all these sources of information we get the rather clear impression that the people of those days were not so very different from the people who live now. They were very much the same kind of beings that are now called men.

In that age which is so well known to us, there lived in a country that we can still visit any day, and at a time which can be approximately fixed, a man who was known as Jesus of Nazareth. It is not denied by any serious historians that this man did live. He lived not at a period of remote antiquity but in historical times, and we can today look out upon the very scenes upon which He looked out, when He walked along the shores of the Lake of Galilee.

What was the origin of the human life of this man, Jesus? Was he descended from previous men by ordinary generation? Was he a product of evolution?

Well, if we had only the kind of evidence that is relied upon to establish the doctrine of evolution with regard to the origin of the first man, we should certainly answer that question in the affirmative; we should certainly say that Jesus of Nazareth most assuredly was descended from previous men by ordinary generation. He did not make upon anyone the impression of being at all abnormal in His appearance. He was amazingly different, indeed, from other men in His character, and in His powers. But I really do not think that there is much doubt but that, if His body as it was when He lived on earth were still somewhere upon earth – which, as a matter of fact, it is not – and if some archaeologist or geologist should discover remains of it in the rocks or in the soil, those remains would show the most thoroughgoing similarity to the bodily structure of previous men.

What inference would be drawn from that if the same kind of reasoning were used as the reasoning which is used when evolutionists argue for the descent of the first man from other forms of animal life? Why, the inference would be drawn that of course Jesus was descended by ordinary generation from the men who lived before Him on the earth. The evidence of continuity of bodily descent, which in the case of the first man is, after all, very far indeed from being complete, since, to say the least, there are enormous gaps between the remains of man and the remains of other forms of animal life, would in the case of the man Jesus seem to be absolutely complete. The proof would seem to be overwhelming.

Yet, despite all that evidence, we hold, on the testimony of the first chapter of Matthew and the first chapter of Luke, that Jesus was not as a matter of fact descended from previous men by ordinary generation, but that at the beginning of His life upon this earth there was a creative act of God, the supernatural conception in the womb of the virgin Mary. Not even the body of Jesus, to say nothing of His human soul, was produced, then, according to our belief, merely by evolution, merely by ordinary generation in the ordinary course of nature, but it was produced also by a supernatural act of God. There you have an instance of special creation right in the full light of historical times.

Of course, a great many people deny that that Biblical narrative of the virgin birth is true. 'You are wrong,' they tell us, 'in holding that Jesus was conceived by the Holy Ghost in the womb of the virgin Mary. As a matter of fact He was just the child of Joseph; He was a product of ordinary generation after all.'

All right, I know that people say that. I know perfectly well that many people deny the virgin birth of Christ. But my point is that when they deny it, and when in denying it they reject the view about it that I hold, they cannot rule me out of court on the ground that I lack some vast fund of expert knowledge that they possess. They cannot say to me, as evolutionists say to me regarding the origin of the first man: 'You have not a sufficient knowledge of biology and of geology to give you a right to have an opinion; we are the experts in this field, and as experts we tell you that Jesus was the son of Joseph by ordinary generation.' If they said that, they would only make themselves ridiculous. Obviously the question is one about which the biological expert is not one tiny little bit more competent to judge than is the plain man. Similarity of bodily structure between Jesus and the men who lived before Him on the earth is admitted by everyone. Yet despite that similarity of bodily structure, we hold, on the basis of what we regard as adequate testimony, that Jesus was not descended from previous mankind by ordinary generation, but that at the origin of His human life there was an entrance, into the course of the world, of the immediate power of God.

But if there was an entrance of the immediate power of God in connection with the origin of the human life of Jesus, why may there not have been also an entrance of the immediate power of God in the case of the first man who ever appeared upon the earth? If similarity of bodily structure does not disprove the occurrence of the miracle in the one case, why should it do so in the other?

I am indeed perfectly well aware of the fact that there is a great difference between the two cases – not only a difference between the men who appeared in each case as a result of the supernatural act of God (Adam being man and man only, and Jesus being God and man), but also a difference in the supernatural act of God itself. I do not for a minute admit that the beings who lived before the first man upon this earth were as much like that first man in external appearance as the men who lived before our Lord were like our Lord in external appearance. I hold that the immense gaps which admittedly exist in the evidence for continuity between the lower animals and man are highly significant and I do not believe that they will ever be filled up.

But the point I am making is that the real decision as to what view is to be held about the origin of the first man is not reached by a consideration of the evidence adduced by biologists or by geologists. If it were reached by a consideration of such evidence, possibly the plain man might be held not to have a right to an opinion about it. It might then seem to be a question to be fought out by experts, with the plain man meekly accepting whatever verdict the experts might bring forth. But as a matter of fact the decision is reached on the basis of other kinds of evidence, which are just as much within the competence of the plain man as they are within the competence of experts.

Is there a God, Creator and Ruler of the world? Is He free to enter in creative fashion into the world that He has made? Has He actually so entered in creative fashion in the Person of Jesus Christ and in the miracles recorded in the Bible?

If a negative answer is given to these questions, then no doubt the evolutionary view will be held regarding the origin of man. The biological and geological evidence obviously does not of itself justify such a view. There are, to say the least, stupendous gaps in the evidence, and the relevance of the evidence may be seriously questioned. Ob-

[123]

viously a leap must be taken before the evolutionary hypothesis is accepted. But that leap will seem to be almost a matter of course to the man who does not believe in a transcendent personal God eternally free as over against the world that He has made, or to the man who does not believe that in the Person of Jesus Christ God has actually entered by an immediate, supernatural action into the course of the world.

On the other hand, to the person who does not share those naturalistic presuppositions, that leap from the actual evidence to the evolutionary hypothesis will seem to be a reckless leap indeed. To the person who does not believe that Jesus Christ was a product of evolution, but who believes that He came into this world by a stupendous miracle, the testimony to an equally supernatural origin of the first man will seem to be overwhelming. Such a person will say with great confidence, not that man is a product of evolution but that God created man.

11: How Did God Create Man?

IN THE LAST OF THESE LITTLE TALKS I SPOKE TO you about the question, 'Did God create man?' Today I want to speak to you about the question, 'How did God create man?'

The answer to that question that is given in the Shorter Catechism of the Presbyterian churches is as follows: 'God created man male and female, after his own image, in knowledge, righteousness, and holiness, with dominion over the creatures.' The Westminster Confession of Faith, making a little more explicit one thing that is implied in the Shorter Catechism, says that God 'created man, male and female, with reasonable and immortal souls'. I want to speak to you first about that very important thing.

Unquestionably the Bible recognizes the presence of two distinct principles or substances in man – his body and his soul.

That is made plain in the first book of the Bible, where, in the account of the creation of man, it is said: 'And the Lord God formed man of the dust of the ground, and breathed into his nostrils the breath of life; and man became a living soul.' But it is so pervasive throughout the Bible that any citation of individual passages in support of it would seem to be almost superfluous. When Jesus makes the distinction between soul and body in His solemn words: 'And fear not them which kill the body, but are not able to kill the soul: but rather fear him which is able to destroy both soul and body in hell,'[1] He is only making

[1] Matt. 10:28.

explicit what really underlies all the teaching of the Word of God.

The Bible does not, indeed, teach that it is desirable for the soul to be separated from the body; it does not encourage at all the Greek notion that the body is the prison-house of the soul, and that a disembodied state is a state of freedom for which we ought to long. On the contrary, it teaches very plainly that the connection between soul and body is the normal and desirable thing and that a disembodied state is a state of nakedness from which the Christian desires to be delivered. Thus the Christian doctrine of the resurrection of the body is very different from the Greek doctrine of the immortality of the soul.

Nevertheless the Bible does teach that the soul is a substance distinct from the body, and that it may exist, and in the case of those who die before the return of Christ and the last judgment, actually does exist, separate from the body.

In thus affirming the existence of the soul, the Bible is in direct conflict with many powerful tendencies in modern unbelief. Great hosts of unbelievers deny not only the existence of a personal God but also the existence of the human soul. Indeed the two denials are very closely related. It is a true saying which declares that if one does not believe that there is a soul in the little world of man's life, neither is he likely to believe that there is any God in the great world of the universe.

The most thoroughgoing way of denying the existence of the soul is found in the doctrine of materialism, which has been expressed picturesquely in the dictum that the brain secretes thought as the liver secretes bile.

I wonder whether you ever felt the depressing pull of that doctrine, as I did in one period of my life.

There is something rather uncanny, is there not, in the close connection between the mind and the brain? Certain mental functions have been shown to be connected with certain areas of the brain. Injure those brain areas, and those mental functions cease. Does not that show, then, that all mental functions are just forms of physical reaction – particularly intricate forms of physical reaction, no doubt, but still forms of physical reaction all the same?

Touch a sensitive plant, and the plant curls up. No mental activity on the part of the plant is involved. Now certain reactions on the part of animals and of men seem to be not essentially different. There is some sense-stimulus; that is transmitted to the brain by the sensory nerves; an impulse is immediately transmitted from the brain to the muscles, and an action immediately follows. It looks as though it were all just a particularly delicate piece of machinery.

In the case of some sense-stimuli the action does not so immediately follow. Light rays coming from a printed page impinge on the retina of the eye; the optic nerve transmits the impression to the brain; nothing then seems to happen. We say the man is reading. He goes on sitting quietly in his chair; he does not seem to react in any immediate way to those sense impressions.

Sometimes I confess I have difficulty in avoiding an immediate reaction. There are some forms of tommy-rot so outrageous that when I come across such tommy-rot on the printed page I feel as though I ought to do something about it at once. But I restrain myself. I go on sitting quietly in my chair; I do not curl up like a sensitive plant; I do not kick as I do when a doctor hits me on my crossed knee to see whether my nerves are in the proper condition. I just seem to do nothing about it.

But, says the materialist, an impression has been made

THE CHRISTIAN VIEW OF MAN

on my brain nevertheless. That tommy-rot on the printed page has left its mark in my brain. After reading it I shall never be the same again. The physical impression in the brain is too minute to be detected by the most powerful microscope; but it is there, and at some time – perhaps years afterwards – it may have its effect upon my conduct. The brain, in other words, has the faculty of recording impressions in a physical way, like impressions made upon a phonograph record, and at some future time the record thus made may be run off.

All right, that is beautifully simple, is it not? All disconcerting factors have been removed. The whole universe has been brought under the unified reign of a law of conservation of physical energy.

Of course, some questions may conceivably be asked by us ignorant folk. All the physical actions of man have been beautifully explained by the materialistic theory; they have all been explained as being due ultimately to physical impressions made upon the brain. But then is not one thing forgotten? How about thought; how about consciousness? Is not this rather a curious piece of mechanism after all? Is a machine, no matter how intricate, aware of itself and aware of the world about it? Must not this therefore be something more than a machine? Must not the mind be something rather different from the brain?

Well, the materialist does not give any serious attention to such ignorant questions as that. Of course, he admits that there is this curious concomitant of certain brain-phenomena which we call consciousness or thought. We do not know exactly what to do with it. We cannot look at it through the microscope; we cannot weigh it in a chemical balance. But we ought not to bother much about it. A thing that cannot be looked at through the microscope and cannot be weighed in a chemical balance is certainly not scientifically respectable. It has no effect on the mighty process of nature. That goes smoothly on under the law of the conservation of energy quite regardless of this strange will-o'-the-wisp of consciousness that plays meaninglessly around some of its operations. No, we ought not to trouble our heads about such a very intangible something-or-other as that. 'Bane and blessing, pain and pleasure' – these things may be all very well for poets and children; but they ought to be quite beneath the attention of scientific men.

Such is the attitude of the materialist. There is a certain strange fascination about it; it possesses the fascination of simplicity. I remember, as I say, that there was a time in my life when I was troubled by it. But then I read Ward's *Naturalism and Agnosticism* and other books and succeeded in getting out of it. Or, rather, God graciously delivered me from the abyss.

The truth is, the simplicity of materialism is a baneful simplicity. It is the simplicity which is arrived at by an ignoring of some of the facts. Every problem becomes simple if you treat it in that way – if, that is, you ignore those elements in it that will not fit into some preconceived view regarding the solution.

Chess problems are somewhat similar. You think you have the solution of the problem: 'White to play and mate in three moves!' You make what you think is the best move for White; then you try over what you think are all the moves that Black might make; then you meet them all by devastating moves on the part of White. And so poor Black goes straight on to his doom. At White's third move Black seems inevitably to be checkmated. You think you have solved the problem; you think that as a solver of chess problems you are really pretty good. But then you look at the problem a little closer, and you discover that Black had a perfectly good answer to that first move of White. He had a knight or castle or bishop which could be moved so as to ward off the threatened attack.

Well, what do you do when you discover that possible move of Black? Do you stick to your solution of the problem all the same? Do you say: 'It was a mighty good solution, and I am just going to stick to it by ignoring that disconcerting move of Black that broke it up.' Not at all! You cannot do that at all. There is no such thing as 'nearly right' in a chess problem. That one disconcerting move of Black broke up your solution just as completely as if there had been a dozen moves like that. Just because of the possibility of that one move for Black, you have to make an entirely different first move for White. You have to begin all over again.

So it is with the materialist and his easy solution of the problem of the universe. He has his solution all nicely worked out. It is a very neat little solution. It seems to be quite beautiful in its simplicity. It seems to be quite worthy of being listed among the successful solutions in tomorrow's newspaper column.

But then I come along and point out to him the fact that his solution ignores the presence, as one of the factors in the problem, of mind or consciousness or thought.

What does he say when I point that out to him? Well, perhaps he says he does not like the thing that I have pointed out to him. He is a scientist, he says; and it is beneath his dignity to deal with such an imponderable thing as consciousness or mind.

What do I then say to him? Well, I am afraid I am rather hard-boiled about the matter. I say to him: 'Yes,

I know that you do not like this imponderable thing that is called consciousness. I do not wonder that you do not like it, because it demolishes your whole solution of the problem of the universe. I am really awfully sorry for you, old man. It must be very disappointing to have to start out in the solution of the problem all over again. But then, you see, I really cannot help it. After all, we have to take the facts as we find them. We cannot get rid of any of them because we do not like them. As a scientific man, you surely ought to recognize that.'

Such might be the answer that I might render to the materialist. I hope you do not think that in making that answer I am falling into that same undue simplicity with which I charged my opponent in the debate. I do not for a moment claim that with my solution of the problem of the universe, which I am seeking to substitute for the solution of the materialist, I have answered all possible questions and removed all mysteries. But still I do make bold to say rather confidently that, whatever my solution of the problem may be, no solution is satisfactory which does not take account of the reality of consciousness or mind.

Indeed, when you come to think of it, is not the reality of consciousness or mind even more certain than the existence of the material world? After all, is not consciousness or mind the thing that we are aware of most clearly of all?

I confess that I have a certain sympathy for the position of the idealist at this point. The materialist says that matter is the only reality. Then comes along the idealist and says: 'No, the only reality is mind.' I say I have a certain sympathy for him when he says that. I do not say that I agree with him. But I have a certain sympathy for him. I can see that he is under a delusion; but at least I can understand how he 'got that way'.

You see, the thing that we know most immediately of all is our own mind. I may say, indeed, that I perceive other things beside what is in my own mind; I say I perceive a microphone there in front of me in this broadcasting station. To adapt the words of Mark Twain, 'it looks like a microphone, it's located like a microphone, and . . . if I don't believe it *is* a microphone'. So I reason, if I reason like Mark Twain's blue jay in investigating his hole in the roof, and so I reason also if I reason like the ordinary American citizen.

But then along comes the idealistic philosopher, and *he* reasons very differently. 'You say you see a microphone there in front of your eyes,' he says to me. 'Well, you don't mean to tell me that you think that microphone really exists.' I am a little alarmed at this point. Is there anything wrong with me? Am I 'seeing things'? I am almost afraid to answer. But finally I pluck up courage. 'Yes, sir,' I say, 'I did think it was a real microphone.' 'How do you know it is a real microphone?' says he. 'Because I see it,' I say. 'There it is; it is a perfectly good brown-coloured microphone.' At this point, my idealist philosopher friend gives a chuckle. He evidently thinks he has me where he wants me. 'What is that you said?' he asks. 'Did you say that the microphone is brown? Well, what do you mean by "brown"? Suppose that microphone had always been in a perfectly dark place, and never could by any possibility be anywhere except in a perfectly dark place; and suppose, furthermore, that there were not and never could be anybody to look at the microphone, would there be any meaning in saying that the microphone was brown or black or white? Is not the colour of the microphone, then, really

How Did God Create Man?

something in the observer's mind and not something that
belongs to the microphone itself?'

Well, I begin to think it over, and perhaps come to the
conclusion that there may be something in what my philosopher friend is saying. The colour of the microphone does
perhaps seem to be something that is in the mind of the
observer rather than something that belongs to the microphone itself. But then a bright thought strikes me. Am I
not aware of the existence of that microphone in other
ways than through the sense of sight? 'Why,' I say to my
idealist friend, 'I know that microphone exists because I
can reach out and touch it. There! I have touched it. It is
hard, and it has a certain size because it takes me a certain
time to move my finger over it from side to side. Now, my
philosopher friend, what are you going to do with that? You
cannot possibly reduce anything as hard and as big as that
microphone is to a mere idea in my mind. A person cannot
stump his toe on an idea. If I stump my toe on a thing or
feel it with my hand I know that it is not an idea in my
mind but something that does sure enough exist.'

But those philosophers are mighty hard to silence in
an argument. You may stump your toe, but you cannot
stump a philosopher. They have an answer to everything.
And so my idealist philosopher friend is not a bit impressed by my appeal from the sense of sight to the sense
of touch. 'After all,' he says, 'the senses from the philosopher's point of view are all essentially alike, and they
are all equally untrustworthy. When I say that I touch that
microphone, all that I am really aware of is a certain sen-
sation in my mind. As a philosopher I really cannot go
beyond that. So if there *were* an external world independent of my mind I could never know what it is in itself.
How then do I know such an external world exists? I do

[133]

not really know it at all. Mind, therefore, is the only reality.'

So says the idealist philosopher about the problem of mind and matter. What do you say about the idealist philosopher? Well, I am afraid some of you may be unkind enough to say a plenty about him. I am afraid some of you may be unkind enough to say that he is completely 'nutty'. Why should we devote our attention to 'nuts' like him?

Now possibly you are nearly right about the idealist philosopher. I am not saying you are not. But then, you see, when a form of insanity becomes as prevalent as this idealistic philosophy, with its attendant scepticism about the existence of an external world, has become in the course of human history, and when it dominates whole ages and percolates down from the philosophers and the poets until it touches the plain man's life at a thousand points, why then I think some attention ought to be given to it by everyone who loves his fellow men.

Of course I am bound to say that in its consistent form – the form in which alone anything very plausible can be said for it – it can easily be shown to involve consequences that are quite absurd. The solid consideration with which it starts is the difficulty of seeing how I can really be sure of any reality that exists independently of my own mind. But to say that there is no reality except what is in my own mind is quite absurd. It would mean that China, Japan and India never had any existence until those countries came within my consciousness. But, say many idealistic philosophers, there are other minds, and so China, Japan and India existed before they came into my consciousness because they existed in those other minds. Indeed, they existed, and all things exist, and I exist, and you exist, in the mind of God.

Thus is idealism pushed straight on from the absurd but consistent view that things exist only in my mind to the depressing but less obviously absurd pantheism which holds that things exist only in the divine mind.

The trouble is, however, that in taking that step idealistic philosophy has sacrificed everything that makes its view at all plausible. The minute I admit that there are minds other than my own, I have admitted that there is a reality outside of my own mind; and when I have admitted that I have taken the really difficult step and there is not the slightest reason why I should not go on and admit the existence of the whole external world just as the plain man does.

I am afraid, however, that some of you may be impatient with this whole discussion. Is it not high time, you may say, that we should return to common sense? Others of you may want to return to the Bible. Is it not time that we should return to our Bible? you may say. Was not this hour supposed to be devoted to an exposition of what the Bible teaches? And here we are wasting our time on a lot of philosophical subtleties.

I am inclined to have a good deal of sympathy with both of these suggestions. I am perfectly ready to return to common sense, and I am perfectly ready to return to the Bible. And the best of it is that if we do one of these two things, with regard to the subject that we are now dealing with, we shall also do the other.

The Bible is a wonderfully common-sense book. Amid the excesses of philosophers on the right hand and on the left, the Bible goes straight on along the pathway of common sense; and it does not seem to be at all ashamed of doing so. With a certain majestic assurance it confirms the common judgment of mankind that mind is one thing and matter another, and that both truly exist.

But, you may say, how about our initial difficulty? How about the connection between the facts of consciousness and physical changes in the brain? Do you deny that there is some connection?

No, I say, I do not deny that there is some connection. When I engage in the unwonted mental exercise of thinking, I sometimes get a headache from it. I dare say some physical change in my brain always accompanies all my thinking and all my feeling.

But what of it? The materialist explains that connection between physical processes in the brain and thought-processes in the mind by saying that only physical processes exist and that what we call the mind is only a very intricate form of physical process. The explanation is quite absurd, when you come to think of it. But why is there not another perfectly good explanation? Why cannot the connection between brain processes and mind processes be explained equally well just by saying that the mind makes use of the brain as its instrument? That thesis was defended with great force in Thomson's *Brain and Personality* that appeared some years ago. There is really nothing whatever against it.

No doubt the relation between the mind and the brain is a great mystery. Mental processes and physical processes seem to be so utterly disparate. But there are many mysterious things which yet must be accepted as facts. So with great confidence we can accept the teaching of the Bible to the effect that man has a body and also has a soul, and that neither soul nor body is a mere semblance but that both do most truly exist.

12: God's Image in Man

WE SPOKE IN THE LAST TALK ABOUT THE SOUL OF
man. God created man with a body, we say, but He also
created man with a soul.

I think we ought to hold not only that man has a soul,
but that it is important that he should know that he has a
soul.

A good many people seem to think it is not particularly
important. Just study the behaviour of people, they say;
classify your observations; and then seek to get people to
form such habits as will result in behaviour of a kind to
promote the well-being of the race. That, say these men, is
the proper scientific method. In it all introspection, all in-
terrogation by a man of the facts of his own inner life, all
talk about the existence of a soul, and the like, should be
rigorously avoided. Just take human behaviour, study it
as it is, and leave metaphysical or philosophical questions
about the soul or about God rigidly alone!

Such is the method. The strange thing is that some
people who do, I suppose, believe in the existence of the
soul and of God seem to think that this method can safely
be followed as far as it goes. Why may we not accept the
psychological studies of those psychologists who do not
believe in the soul and in God, and then use them in the
propagation of a philosophy and a theology very different
from the scepticism of these men? Why may not the re-
searches of these psychologists be regarded by the Christian as being all right in their own limited sphere?

Such reasoning is very precarious. As a matter of fact,

you cannot well keep one department of knowledge separate from another in such a water-tight compartment as that. No, the views that a man has about the soul and about God will colour his interpretation of the phenomena of human behaviour; and, on the other hand, a false or limited observation of the phenomena of human behaviour will colour what a man thinks about the existence of the soul and the existence of God.

I think, then, that it is not only important that I have a soul, but also important for me to know that I have a soul.

What, then, does it mean when I hold that I have a soul? What does the Bible mean when it tells me that I have one?

For one thing, it means what I spoke to you about in the preceding talk. It means that the materialists are wrong, and that, contrary to their view, the mind or consciousness is something different from the brain.

But it means also something more than that. It means not only that man has mind or consciousness, but also that his mind or consciousness is a unity. It is not a mere stream of consciousness, but the consciousness of a person. Not merely does thinking go on within me, but it is *I* that think. It was I many years ago, and it is the same I today, and it will be the same I to all eternity. That is what the Bible means when it tell me that I have a soul.

It is rather an appalling thing – this terrible isolation of the individual soul. That isolation is expressed by theologians and philosophers in many learned works; but it is also expressed by the cry of the human heart. It is expressed, for example, in words of one syllable in a negro song that I dearly love. Did you ever listen to it in lighter mood as though it were an amusing thing? Well, I think if you listened to it in any such mood, you will say that though you went to laugh you came away to pray. I re-

[138]

member how my mother used to speak of the solemnity with which that song sets forth the loneliness of the soul in the presence of God. 'It's not my father,' the song says in words that I cannot exactly remember, 'it's not my mother, it's not my brother; it's me, O Lord, standin' in the need of prayer.'

There we have the cry of the human soul, in its awful separation from all else, in the awful loneliness of its existence as an indivisible and immortal soul.

That loneliness and indivisibleness of the soul belongs to all sorts and conditions of men. It is one of the things that most clearly constitute us men; it was stamped upon us by the creation once and for all. Even sin does not destroy it, though sin makes it no longer a blessing but an unspeakable horror and curse.

Such, at least in bare outline, is what the Bible means when it says that man has a soul.

At this point it becomes necessary for us to deal, in passing, with one subsidiary question, just in order that the teaching of the Bible regarding the nature of man may stand out in its true simplicity.

We have been saying that according to the Bible man has a body and a soul. But a great many readers of the Bible – some of them not only very learned but also very devout readers – have told us that that is not a complete statement of what the Bible teaches. No, they say, man is composed according to the Bible, not just of body and soul, but of body, soul and spirit. Thus they favour not a two-fold but a threefold division of the nature of man.

People who hold this view differ, no doubt, somewhat as to what constitutes the difference between what they call the soul and what they call the spirit. Some of them have no doubt thought of the 'soul' as simply the principle of animal life – the principle of life which man shares with the lower animals. But I am inclined to think that in the form in which the theory is most prominent today the 'soul' is thought of as comprising faculties of man including some of the faculties of intellect, feeling and will, which are distinctly human faculties, but do not include some still higher part of man's nature by which he enters into communion with God.

But is this theory correct or is it incorrect? Does the Bible really teach that the spirit of man is to be distinguished from his soul, or does it teach that the soul of man and the spirit of man are exactly the same thing, called by two different names?

I think the answer to this question is given with particular clearness in one great passage in the Bible, the passage which is found in the second chapter of the First Epistle to the Corinthians, running into the beginning of the third chapter.

In that passage Paul repeatedly distinguishes the soul from the spirit, and speaks of the man characterized by 'soul' as distinguished from the man characterized by 'spirit'. 'But a soul-man,' he says, 'receiveth not the things of the Spirit of God: for they are foolishness unto him: neither can he know them, because they are spiritually discerned. But the "Spirit-man" judgeth all things, yet he himself is judged of no man.' I have just quoted I Cor. 2: 14f. Probably many of you will say that the quotation is not just exactly right. What the English Bible says is: 'The natural man receiveth not the things of the Spirit of God'. and I think we shall see in a moment that that is really a splendid translation, a translation that comes just about as near to the meaning of the original as any translation into the English language possibly could come. But what the Greek really says instead of 'the natural man' is 'the soulish man' – only we have no such word as 'soulish' in the English language, and so we come as near to the meaning as we possibly can when we translate as the Authorized Version of the Bible does at this point.

But if the Bible contrasts the 'soulish man' or the 'soul-man' with the 'spirit-man' in this passage, have we not here a very clear example of the threefold division of man's nature, the division not just into body and soul but into body, soul and spirit? Does not this passage clearly distinguish the spirit of man from the soul of man?

The answer is most emphatically 'No'. On the contrary, this passage distinctly discourages the threefold division of man's nature into body, soul and spirit, and encourages the twofold division into body and soul. The plain fact is that the word 'spirit' in the adjective 'spiritual' used in the phrase 'the spiritual man' does not refer to the spirit of man at all, but refers to the Spirit of God. I do not see how it would be possible to make that much clearer than this passage makes it. 'For what man knoweth the things of a man,' says the passage in the eleventh verse, 'save the spirit of man which is in him? even so the things of God knoweth no man, but the Spirit of God.' Then the passage goes on to speak about the man who knows the things of God because the Spirit of God is in him.

What then is meant by the 'spirit-man' or the 'spiritual man' as over against the 'soul-man'? Why, the thing is as plain as day. The 'soul-man' is a man who has only a human soul, and the 'spiritual man' is the man who, in addition to his human soul, has the Holy Spirit, the Spirit of God.

How utterly wrong is it then to say that the 'spiritual' man is the man who has developed a higher aspect or part of his own nature, called the 'spirit' as over against the 'soul'! No, the 'spiritual' man is the man who has been transformed by the Holy Spirit, the Spirit of God, the Third Person of the Trinity, and the 'soul-man' is the man who has merely his human soul not so transformed. The key to this passage, as to other passages in the Epistles of Paul, is given if we think of the word 'Spirit' in the adjective 'spiritual' as being spelled with a capital letter because it refers not to the spirit of man but to the Spirit of God.

Very different is the use of the word 'spiritual' in modern religious parlance. I have come almost to hate that word, so terribly is it being misused. It is constantly being used to designate a religious man, a man who has developed some supposedly peculiar religious faculty of his nature as over against other faculties. So it is sometimes said of some unbeliever in the pulpit, if objection is made to the opposition between his preaching and the Word of God: 'Oh, but he is so spiritual!' The meaning is, I suppose, that he is not interested in dollars and cents or in things to eat, but is interested in the things of the human spirit. That is certainly very far indeed from the Biblical sense of the word. In the Biblical sense, the spiritual man is the man who has been begotten again, and has had not a part of his nature but all of his nature transformed by the supernatural act of the Spirit of God.

I think, then, that the threefold division of man's nature into body, soul and spirit is out of accord with the true meaning of that great passage in the second and third chapters of the First Epistle to the Corinthians. But are there not other passages in the Bible which seem to favour that threefold division?

It seems to me that the only passage which can be appealed to with any plausibility as doing so is found in I

Thess. 5:23, where Paul prays that his readers' spirit and soul and body may be kept whole and without blame at the appearance of our Lord Jesus Christ. But certainly that passage cannot rightly be used to overthrow the clear teaching of the rest of the Epistles of Paul and the rest of the Bible. It seems clear that Paul is just using a fulness of expression there to express his hope that the whole being of the Thessalonian readers may be kept so as to stand blameless at the second coming of Christ. He is just heaping up words to express that idea. I think we may say that if there had been other words, in addition to the two words 'soul' and 'spirit', to express the idea, he would have used those other words too.

We ought to reject very firmly, therefore, the view that the nature of man is divided by the Bible into body, soul and spirit. The more I reflect about the matter, the more I am convinced that the view of the threefold nature of man is rather a serious error. It is an error that has been held by a great many devout Christian people, and it has been learnedly and reverently defended; and yet it is a serious error all the same.

It encourages what may be called an 'empty-room' view of the presence of God in the redeemed man – the notion that before a man becomes a Christian he is pretty much all right except that there is one room in him that is vacant, the room that ought to be a temple of God. It encourages, in other words, the notion that what happens when a man becomes a Christian is merely that one part of the man's nature, the 'spiritual' part, a part previously neglected, is developed and given the place which it ought to have in human life.

Such a notion fails to do justice to the teachings of the Bible. The real state of human nature after the fall of man is not that one part of it has been cut off or can attain only a stunted growth, but that all of it is corrupt. The real thing that happens when a man becomes a Christian is not that God is set up and enthroned in a part of man's nature which before was like an empty room, but that the whole man, corrupt before because of sin, is transformed by the regenerating power of the Spirit of God.

I think we ought to be very clear, then, that the Bible does not distinguish the human spirit from the human soul. No doubt these two words designate the same thing in two different ways, and it would be interesting to study the difference between them; but the important thing to observe now is that they do designate the same thing. They are just two different words to designate what we can call in English either man's soul or man's spirit, and which, in order to avoid confusion, we shall now speak of as man's soul.

What have we been doing in this discussion? Have we been engaging in undue subtleties that have taken us away from the simplicity of the Bible? On the contrary, I think we have been rubbing away the subtleties with which the interpretation of the Bible at this point has sometimes been overloaded, in order to recover the true simplicity of the Word of God. The Bible presents a view of the nature of man which is very simple. Man, according to the Bible, has a body and he has a soul. I think we ought to return to that simple Biblical teaching.

When we do return to it, we are in a position to consider its implications. No longer distracted by any attempt to distinguish man's soul from man's spirit, we can go on to envisage the great mystery which the Bible designates by both of these words.

That mystery is set forth by the Bible when it tells us that God made man in His own image. 'So God created man,' says the Bible, 'in his own image, in the image of God created he him; male and female created he them.'[1]

The 'image of God' cannot well refer to man's body, because God is a spirit; it must therefore refer to man's soul. It is man's soul which is made in the image or likeness of God.

But what was there in man's soul, as he was created, which was like God? Well, one important element in that likeness has already been set forth. God is a person, or, rather, three persons in one God, and man is a person. In that, man is like God.

What a stupendous mystery that is! Here is man, a finite creature, product of God's creative hand, walking here upon this earth in a body made of the dust of the ground. Yet this being, so contemptible as he might at first sight seem, possesses the strange and terrible gift of personal freedom, and is capable of personal companionship with the infinite and eternal God. That the Bible certainly means when it says that God created man in His own image.

But is that all that it means?

Some have said so. Some have said that the image of God in man means not that man as created was in any respect the same kind of person as God is, but simply and solely that he was a person. It does not, say these men, involve any moral likeness between man as created and God.

Those who have said that may be divided into two classes.

In the first place, there are those who have said that man before he fell into sin was simply neutral with respect to good and evil. He was free, and that was all. He was neither

[1] Gen. 1:27.

good nor bad, and it was for him to determine whether he would become good or bad. He had not made any choices between good and evil. If he made good choices he would become good; if he made bad choices he would become bad: but as created by God he was neither one nor the other. He was like God simply because he had personal freedom: and personal freedom, not goodness, is what the Bible means by the image of God.

That view involves a very deadly error. It involves the deadly error in which the will of a free person is represented as swinging in a sort of vacuum undetermined by any character of the person as either good or bad. The Bible holds no such view. The Bible says: 'Out of the abundance of the heart the mouth speaketh,'[1] and: 'A good tree cannot bring forth evil fruit, neither can a corrupt tree bring forth good fruit.'[2] According to the Bible good actions come from a good person and evil actions come from an evil person; according to the Bible, goodness and badness do not inhere simply in individual conscious actions but inhere also in something that lies far deeper than individual actions. If we are true to the Bible, we cannot possibly speak of a person who is neither good nor bad; we cannot speak of a person who is morally neutral, whose moral quality is left to be determined by his own future choices, being good only as each individual action is good and bad only as each individual action is bad. We ought to get rid of that whole notion in a very radical way.

Other theologians have held a view similar to the one of which we have just spoken, but have endeavoured to avoid some of its most obviously wrong implications.

Man as created, they have held, was morally neutral. In

[1] Matt. 12:34.   [2] Matt. 7:18.

saying that they say something that is like the view of which we have just spoken. The image of God in which the Bible says man was created means, say these theologians, simply personal freedom, not goodness. But then, these theologians say, God at once gave to man – distinct from his creation – a supernatural gift of goodness, which was necessary in order that harmony in his appetites should be secured. When man fell by sinning against God, what happened was simply that that supernatural and additional gift of goodness was lost, but the image of God, which consisted simply in the nature of man as a free person, remained intact.

That view also is very wrong. It involves a shallow view of sin, and it is quite contrary to the teaching of the Word of God.

No, when the Bible tells us that man was created in the image of God, it means more than that man had personal freedom. That, indeed, is a necessary element in what the Bible means by the image of God; but that is not all that the Bible means by the image of God. The Bible means also that man as created was like God in that he was good. He was not, as created, morally neutral – indeed the whole notion of a morally neutral person is a monstrosity – but his nature was positively directed to the right and opposed to the wrong. Goodness was not something accidental, something that came in after man was created; but it was something that was stamped upon him in the very act of creation by the Creator's hand. About man as about all the rest of the creation the Bible says: 'And God saw every thing that he had made, and, behold, it was very good.'[1]

Yet man fell. How great a fall was that! It was not

[1] Gen. 1: 31.

merely the loss of a gift not part of man's original being, but it was the loss of something that belonged from the beginning to the very image of God in man. How sadly was God's image marred! We must speak of that in the next of these talks.

13: The Covenant of Life

WE OBSERVED IN THE LAST TALK THAT WHEN THE
Bible says God created man in His own image, that means
something more than that man as created was a person as
God is a person. The image of God in man does mean that,
but it means far more than that. It also means that there
was a moral likeness between man and God. Man as created, in other words, was like God not only in that he
was a person but also in that he was good.

We saw that that view of the image of God in man,
denied though it is by erroneous ways of thinking of various kinds, is supported by certain very powerful considerations drawn from the entire way in which the Bible speaks
of the creation of man. But it is also supported by two New
Testament passages to which particular attention ought
now to be paid. These passages are found in the third chapter of the Epistle to the Colossians and in the fouth chapter of the Epistle to the Ephesians.

In Colossians 3:10, Paul speaks of his readers as having
put off the old man and as having 'put on the new man
which is renewed unto knowledge after the image of him
that created him.' Here we have a mention of the image
of God. What light does the passage shed upon the question what the image of God means?

No doubt the direct reference here is not to the first
creation of man, which we are studying just now, but to
the new creation which takes place when a man becomes a
Christian – that new creation which is essentially the same

thing as that which is spoken of elsewhere in the Bible as the new birth.

But although the direct reference is to the new creation, there is the plainest possible allusion to the first creation, the very words of Genesis 1:27 being in part used; and in particular we learn from this passage something very important about what the image of God in that Genesis passage means. The image of God, which is here mentioned in Colossians, is plainly intended to be essentially the same as the image of God which is spoken of in the Genesis passage.

Very well, then. By examining what Paul here says about the image of God we can learn something about what is meant by that phrase in Genesis 1:27.

What, then, does our examination of the Pauline passage show? Why, it shows that the 'image of God' as the Bible means it includes knowledge. 'Having put on the new man,' says Paul, 'which is renewed *unto knowledge* after the image of him that created him.'

But that word knowledge is unquestionably a very rich term. The knowledge of which Paul is speaking, and which he here says to be part of the image of God in man, is not merely intellectual knowledge like that which the demons have when they tremble before God, but it includes also a true apprehension of God such as only they possess who stand in communion with Him. Such knowledge therefore must have been part also of the image of God in which man was first created according to the Book of Genesis.

I do not mean that the redeemed people of God, the people who have passed through the new creation or the new birth, have not more knowledge of God than Adam had when he was first created; indeed they certainly do have much more. But all the same we do obtain from this passage in Colossians very clear information to the effect that the Scriptural idea of the image of God, in which the Book of Genesis says that man was originally created, includes a knowledge which is a truly moral as well as intellectual possession.

The other New Testament passage to which I call your attention is Ephesians 4:24. In that passage Paul speaks of his readers as having so learned Christ that they have put on the new man, 'which after God hath been created in righteousness and holiness of truth'. Here as in the Colossians passage Paul is speaking of the new creation, by which men become Christians, and not directly of the first creation of man narrated in the Book of Genesis. But here as in the Colossians passage there is a clear allusion to that first creation of man and clear light is shed upon it. The words which the English Bible translates 'after God' clearly mean 'according to God', 'with God as a model'. Thus the passage clearly teaches that a man who is created 'with God as a model', or – to express exactly the same idea with other words – who is created after the image of God, necessarily possesses righteousness and holiness. Thus when the Book of Genesis says that God created man in His own image that is shown to mean – if we may interpret Scripture by the aid of Scripture – that God created man in righteousness and holiness.

How utterly the plainly intended parallel between the new creation and the first creation would break down if the image of God were to be interpreted in entirely different senses in the two cases – as involving righteousness and holiness in the case of the new creation and as involving the mere gift of personal freedom without moral quality in the case of the first creation! No, nothing so inconsequential as that is meant. When the Bible speaks of being like God as the high ideal for man – as Jesus, for example, said, 'Be ye therefore perfect, even as your Father which is in heaven is perfect'[1] – it is thinking primarily of moral likeness. So moral likeness is certainly not excluded when the first book of the Bible tells us that God created man in His own image.

The Shorter Catechism, then, is entirely right when it says, in answer to the question, 'How did God create man?': 'God created man male and female, after his own image, in knowledge, righteousness, and holiness, with dominion over the creatures.'

Well, we have got that far anyway, in our account of God's dealings with man. Man was created in knowledge, righteousness and holiness.

But did God leave man alone, after He had thus created him? No, He did not leave him alone; He entered into a covenant with him.

That was, of course, only one thing that He did with man. By His works of providence He preserved and governed man and all his actions as He preserved and governed all His creatures. But the Shorter Catechism is right in singling out that formation of a covenant with man as a 'special act of providence' that God exercised 'towards man, in the estate wherein he was created'.

Now the Bible does not actually use the word 'covenant' at this particular point. Yet the arrangement which it does describe is so similar to other arrangements where it actually uses that term that we can hardly deny to the theologians the right to use the term here. Plainly God did, according to the Book of Genesis, enter into what, according to Scriptural language elsewhere used, was a covenant.

Now when the Bible speaks of a 'covenant' in a connec-

[1] Matt. 5:48.

tion like this, where God was one of the parties, it does not mean exactly what we often in ordinary parlance mean by that term. We mean by a 'covenant', or in more modern language a 'contract', an arrangement which either party is free to enter into or not as it pleases. The Bible does not mean such an ordinary covenant or contract when it uses the term to designate an arrangement between God and man. The reason is that man, though one of the parties, has no choice whatever as to whether he will enter into the arrangement or not. At least, he certainly has no freedom of proposing any other arrangement to put into its place. He has no power to say to God: 'No, I refuse to enter into such an arrangement with you; here is what I propose instead; you can take the contract that I offer you or else we shall just make no contract at all.' He might say that to some human contracting party, but he cannot say that to God.

No, God remains absolutely sovereign, in His covenants as in everything else that He does. Man does not contract with Him on anything in the remotest degree resembling equality. The covenant is an expression of God's will, not man's, and man must listen to its terms, trust God that they are holy and just and good, and order his life accordingly.

What is there, then, about these Biblical covenants that causes the Bible to use the term 'covenant' with regard to them? I think the answer is rather plain. It is that these covenants involve a promise on the part of God – a promise with a condition. God does engage to fulfil His part of the arrangement. He was not obliged so to engage; He was perfectly free not to do so: but when He has once done so, when He has once established the covenant, His honour is involved in the fulfilment of His part of it.

So it was in the case of that covenant into which God

entered with man in the estate wherein He had created him. God entered into it freely: He was not under obligation to enter into it, except in the sense in which all God's actions are determined by the infinite goodness of His own being. But although He entered into it freely, and not under any sort of pressure from or obligation to the other party, man, yet when He had once entered into it man could be quite sure that He would fulfil His part of it to the full.

What, then, were the terms of that covenant into which God entered with man? The terms of it were very simple indeed. If man kept perfectly the commands of God, God would give him life. That was the covenant.

It is true, the Bible does not describe the covenant in just exactly that way. It does not describe it in positive terms but only in negative terms, and it does not describe it in general terms but only by the presentation of a concrete example of the kind of conduct on the part of man that would deprive man of the benefits of the covenant. Here is what the Bible says:[1]

'And the Lord God commanded the man, saying, Of every tree of the garden thou mayest freely eat:

But of the tree of the knowledge of good and evil, thou shalt not eat of it: for in the day that thou eatest thereof thou shalt surely die.'

But although the covenant is directly put only in a negative form, the positive implications are perfectly clear. When God established death as the penalty of disobedience, that plainly meant that if man did not disobey he would have life. Underlying the establishment of the penalty there is clearly a promise.

[1] Gen. 2:16 f.

[154]

Moreover, the one prohibition which God expressly mentioned – the prohibition against eating of the tree of the knowledge of good and evil – is plainly put as a test of man's obedience in general.

The Shorter Catechism, therefore, is fully justified in speaking of this covenant as 'a covenant of life' into which God entered with man, 'forbidding him to eat of the tree of the knowledge of good and evil, upon the pain of death'.

The question then arises, what is meant by 'life', which God promised to man in this 'covenant of life' into which He entered with him, and what is meant by the 'death' which was to be the punishment of disobedience?

In answer to that question I think we ought decidedly to say that the life and the death here spoken of include physical life and physical death. The Bible does seem rather clearly to teach that if man had not disobeyed the command of God his body would not have died, he would not have passed through that dissolution between soul and body which is brought about by the death of a man who has lived upon this earth. I think the fifth chapter of Romans as well as the Book of Genesis teaches that rather plainly.

It is another question in just what way that preservation of life would have been accomplished. Would it have been accomplished because man's body, as created, was not at all subject to death – was not at all subject to that process of decay which now runs through all nature? I am not quite sure that the Bible requires us to say that. It is true, there are in the Bible, in the eighth chapter of the Epistle to the Romans, some very mysterious words regarding what may be called the cosmic effects of sin. They may fairly be held to mean that if sin had not entered, the whole course of the world and not merely of human life would have been very different from what it now is. Paul speaks of the creation as being now subject to the bondage of corruption and as groaning and travailing in pain together until now and as being destined to be delivered from this bondage of corruption into the liberty of the glory of the children of God.[1] What is particularly noteworthy about this passage for our present purpose is not that it promises a glorious transformation of the created world in the future. That is promised elsewhere in Scripture. Isaiah, for example, speaks of the time when there shall be a new heaven and a new earth.[2] But the thing that is especially noteworthy is that Paul seems so clearly to connect the present imperfect condition of the world with sin. That is in accord with what the Book of Genesis says[3] to the effect that the ground was cursed for Adam's sake and that it should bring forth thorns and thistles to him, the sinner. These passages do seem to indicate that the course of nature would have been different if sin had not entered into the world.

Yet I think we might perhaps be going beyond what is written if we said that except for sin the body of man as originally created, and as it would have been found in Adam's posterity, would have had the natural faculty without further change of being free from death. There are no doubt certain difficulties in the way of such a view as that. I will not say whether they are insuperable or not. At any rate it seems to me that we are not necessarily running counter to the teaching of Scripture if we hold that the prevention of death, if Adam had not sinned, would have taken place in some way other than by the operation of the course of nature. Would Adam perhaps have passed through some kind of transformation or translation before

[1] Rom. 8:19–22.   [2] Isa. 65:17.   [3] Gen. 3:17 f.

his body would have become immortal? We simply do not know.

Yet even if we think of the matter in some such way as that which I have just suggested as possible, we still, I suppose, feel rather keenly the clash between this Biblical teaching and the ideas to which we have become accustomed at the present time. We have become accustomed to a view of nature which practically, though not necessarily in theory, ignores God, which universalizes our observations of the course of nature as we now know it and ignores the fact that the Creator of nature still lives and can do what He will with the work of His hands. On the basis of that view into which we have fallen, it seems to some people incredible that man as created should not pass through those processes of decay and death which we now see operative everywhere in the world where life, whether vegetable or animal, is to be found.

But let us look at the thing for the moment from the Christian point of view. We Christians expect, do we not, the resurrection of the body; we look for a life of man, in the body, that shall have no end. Why, then, should we regard as impossible for Adam, had he not sinned, that which we firmly expect for ourselves, as redeemed? Perhaps, indeed, you may object that even Christians will die; their bodies are not exempt, then, from the processes of decay which run all through the natural world. Yes, we reply, but not all Christians will die; those Christians will not die who are alive at the second coming of our Lord. They will be transformed without passing through any dissolution of soul and body in death. We return, then, to our analogy. Why should it be thought a thing incredible that God should have preserved Adam from physical death, had he not sinned, if in accordance with His promise He will preserve from physical death some, at least, of those whom He has redeemed from sin by the blood of Christ? There is really no reason why He should not have done so.

I think, then, that we can with great confidence say that if Adam had not sinned he would not have passed through the experience of physical death. There are many things that are mysterious about the way in which that preservation from death might have been accomplished, but about the fact of it I think the Bible allows little doubt. The Bible seems rather clearly to teach that death, even physical death, was the penalty of sin, and that life, even physical life, would have been the result of obedience.

It should be observed, however, very clearly at this point that although physical death was included in the death that was the penalty of sin, and although physical life was included in the life that was to follow upon obedience, yet physical life and physical death do not by any means exhaust the meaning of the life and the death that are here in view. Life, according to the Bible, is not just existence, but it is existence in the presence and with the favour of God; and death is not just the death of the body but it is separation from God and a doom that should fill the heart of man with a nameless dread. Great vistas of blessedness and of woe are here opened out before us. Very tremendous, according to the Bible, is the issue between life and death.

That issue was placed before man in accordance with what the Shorter Catechism calls the 'covenant of life' into which God entered with Adam. That same covenant is also sometimes called the 'covenant of works'. It is rightly so called because by the terms of it man was to have life or death in accordance with what he did. By the terms of the covenant man was placed on probation. No absolute promise of life was given him; but he was to have life only if he obeyed perfectly the commandments of God.

Do you think that probation was to last forever, or do you think that if man had not sinned there would have come a time when his period of probation would have been over?

Well, unquestionably it would remain true to all eternity that *if* man sinned he would die. That is quite clear. But the question is whether there would have come a time when that 'if' would have lost all practical importance because the possibility of man's sinning would have been done away.

That is what I mean when I ask whether man's probation, as described in the second chapter of Genesis, was permanent or temporary.

I think that question can be very clearly answered. The answer is not, indeed, given by the Bible in so many words; but I think the theologians are right in holding that it is clearly implied.

When God had created man, He permitted him to be tested. He permitted temptation to come to him. If man had stood the test successfully, if he had resisted the temptation, do you think that he would have been brought again and again into jeopardy to all eternity? Do you think, in other words, that if he had resisted the temptation he would have been essentially no better off than he was before? Would there have been, in other words, for man always a possibility of a fall, but never a possibility of attaining a state of final security?

The former alternative seems to be contrary not only to the implications of the narrative in Genesis, but also to the analogy of certain other dealings of God with men.

We do know, if we believe the Bible, that there are men

[159]

in whose case the possibility of sinning is gone. Those are the company of the redeemed in heaven.

In what does the Christian hope consist? Does it consist merely in the hope of being given a new chance to obey the commands of God, to have sin removed, and to have set before us all over again in another world the alternative of life and death as it was set before Adam in Paradise?

No Christian, who has any inkling of the true richness of the great and precious promises of God will say that. On the contrary, the Christian hope is the hope of a time when even the possibility of our sinning will be over. It is not the hope then of a return to the condition of Adam before the fall but the hope of an entrance into a far higher condition.

Now do you think that if Adam had not sinned, the entrance to that higher condition would have been closed to him? Do you think that he would have been left to an eternal jeopardy in which the dread possibility of his sinning would ever have been before his eyes?

I do not believe you will think that if you read your Bible with care. No, the probation into which Adam was put was not an eternal probation. It was a temporary probation, and if it had been passed through without sin it would have been followed by an assured blessedness.

Thus that covenant of works into which God entered with man was a gracious thing. It contained, indeed, a possibility of death, but it contained also the promise of assured and eternal life. If the temptation was yielded to, there would be death; but if the temptation was resisted, even the possibility of death would be removed.

14: The Fall of Man

IN THE LAST OF THESE TALKS, I SPOKE TO YOU about the covenant into which God entered with man in the estate wherein he was created. The terms of the covenant were very simple. If man obeyed perfectly the commands of God he was to have life; if he disobeyed, he was to die. That covenant amounted to a probation in which man was put by God.

Just at the close of the talk, we were observing that the probation was not intended to last forever, but was to be replaced, if man passed successfully through it, by a condition of assured blessedness. If that is not said in so many words in Scripture I do maintain that the theologians are right in holding it to be very clearly implied.

If they are right, then we must supplement in rather an important way what we have said about the original state of man.

In the last two talks, we insisted, against erroneous views of various kinds, that man, as created, was positively good. The image of God, in which the Bible tells us man was created, did not consist merely in personal freedom, but it included knowledge, righteousness and holiness. Man, as created, was like God not merely in being a person, but also in being good.

Now, however, we must observe that although man as created was righteous he was not created in the highest state to which he was capable of attaining. He was righteous, but there was in him a possibility of becoming unrighteous. A still higher state remained for him to attain.

It was a state in which the very possibility of his sinning would be removed.

The means used by God to place that higher state before man as a goal to be attained was the issuance to him of a definite command. 'But of the tree of the knowledge of good and evil, thou shalt not eat of it,' said God.[1] That was the test of man's obedience; that was man's probation.

If the probation had been successfully passed through, then man would have been received at once into eternal life. He possessed life before, but then life would have been assured. The 'if' would all have been removed from the promise of life; the victory would have been won; nothing further could ever by any possibility have separated God from His child.

Very different, however, was the result. Man was left, as the Shorter Catechism puts it, to the freedom of his own will, and he made sad use of his freedom. He might have chosen the way of life, but as a matter of fact he chose the way of death; he fell from the estate wherein he was created by sinning against God. It was a sad choice indeed.

When we say that man had free will and that he chose the way of death, we do not mean that his choice was outside of the eternal plan of God. We do not mean that he surprised God when he sinned. On the contrary, the eternal plan of God, as we saw when we dealt with God's decrees, embraces all things that come to pass. Even the sin of man was brought to pass in accordance with the counsel of God's will.

But as we observed when we dealt with that subject, God brings to pass different things in widely different ways. So He brought to pass the fall of man in a way that preserved to the full man's personal freedom and man's

[1] Gen. 2:17.

responsibility. God is not the author of sin. The tempter and man himself were the authors of man's sin. God's righteousness is forever pure. Yet God used even that terrible evil for His own holy purpose; He permitted man to fall.

Do not ask me why He did so. I cannot tell you. That is the eternal mystery of evil; it is to us an insoluble riddle. We must trust God alone for the solution of it.

One thing, however, is clear. Man had no excuse when he fell. He was guilty in the sight of God. Being left to the freedom of his own will, he fell from the estate wherein he was created by sinning against God.

That brings us to an exceedingly important question – the question, 'What is sin?' It is a question that we cannot ignore. From false answers to it have come untold disaster to mankind and to the Church, and in the right answer to it is to be found the beginning of the pathway of salvation.

How shall we obtain the answer to that momentous question? I want to try to tell you something about that in the next talk. But I think we can make a very good beginning by just examining the Biblical account of the way in which sin entered into the world.

That account is given in the Book of Genesis in a very wonderful manner. The language is very simple; the story is told almost in words of one syllable. Yet how profound is the insight which it affords into the depths of the human soul!

'And the Lord God,' says the Bible, 'commanded the man, saying, Of every tree of the garden thou mayest freely eat: but of the tree of the knowledge of good and evil, thou shalt not eat of it: for in the day that thou eatest thereof thou shalt surely die.'

It has been observed that no reason is said to have been

given to Adam to tell him why he should not eat of that tree, and it has been said that that fact is perhaps significant. Eating of the tree was not in itself obviously wrong; the command not to eat of it was not reinforced by any instinct in man's nature. It appeared therefore all the more clearly as a sheer test of obedience. Would man obey God's commands only when he could detect the reason for them, or would he obey them knowing simply that they were God's commands, knowing that because He gave them they had some quite sufficient reason and were holy and just and good? How clearly and simply that is brought out in the narrative in the Book of Genesis!

An equal simplicity and an equal profundity characterize the following narrative – the narrative of the temptation and the fall.

Adam and Eve were in the garden. The serpent said to the woman, 'Yea, hath God said, Ye shall not eat of every tree of the garden?'

I think we can detect even there the beginnings of the temptation. The woman is asked to eye the things that God has forbidden as though they were desirable things. It is hinted that the commands are hard commands; it is hinted that possibly they might even have involved the prohibition to eat of any of the trees of the garden.

Or else perhaps an attempt is made to cast doubt upon the very fact of the command. '*Hath* God said?' says the tempter. The woman is asked to envisage God's commands as a barrier which it would be desirable to surmount. Is there no loophole? Has God really commanded this and that? Did He really mean to prohibit the eating of the trees of the garden?

The woman's reply states the fact – certainly in the main. God's command did not prohibit the eating of all

[164]

the trees in the garden, but only of one tree. 'And the woman said unto the serpent, We may eat of the fruit of the trees of the garden: but of the fruit of the tree which is in the midst of the garden, God hath said, Ye shall not eat of it, neither shall ye touch it, lest ye die.'

Then at last there comes a direct attack upon the truthfulness of God. 'Ye shall not surely die,' said the tempter. 'Thou shalt surely die,' said God: 'Ye shall not surely die,' said the tempter. At last the battle is directly joined. God, said the tempter, has lied, and He has lied for the purpose of keeping something good from man. 'Ye shall not surely die,' said the tempter: 'for God doth know that in the day ye eat thereof, then your eyes shall be opened, and ye shall be as God, knowing good and evil.'

At that point the question arises in our minds what the element of truth was in those words of the tempter. Those words were a lie, but the truly devilish lies are those that contain an element of truth, or, rather, they are those lies that twist the truth so that the resulting lie looks as though it itself were true.

Certainly it was true that by eating the forbidden fruit Adam attained a knowledge that he did not possess before. That seems to be indicated in verse 22 of the same chapter of the Book of Genesis, where we read: 'And the Lord God said, Behold, the man is become as one of us, to know good and evil.' Yes, it does seem to have been true that when he ate of the forbidden fruit man came to know something that he had not known before.

He had not known sin before; now he knew it. He had known only good before; now he knew good and evil. But what a curse that new knowledge was, and what an immense loss of knowledge as well as loss of everything else that new knowledge brought in its train!

He now knew good and evil; but, alas, he knew good now only in memory, so far as his own experience was concerned; and the evil that he knew he knew to his eternal loss. Innocence, in other words, was gone.

At that point the question naturally arises in our minds whether innocence was the highest state for man. Is a goodness that is good merely because there has never been any knowledge of evil the highest form of goodness? Or is that goodness still higher which has maintained itself in the very face of evil?

Well, I think we ought to be very cautious about answering that question, and I do not think we ought to adopt any answer which will involve making evil a necessary means to the production of good. That would be a very deadly error indeed; for if evil is necessary that there should be good, if good could never exist unless evil were also present, then evil would in some sort cease to be evil and would become itself a kind of good. Indeed, in that case – if evil is necessary to good – evil must be thought of as having a place in the life of God Himself before the creation of the world; and that is the abyss of blasphemy.

But I think we may say that for man as he was actually created, and with evil already present in the world of created beings, resistance to temptation was a pathway to a higher level of perfection than was that innocence in which he was created.

I do not mean that it is ever right to seek temptation in order that we may show how finely we can resist it. The thought of doing that is one of the most often used snares of the devil. A man who is dissatisfied with what Satan calls childish innocence and deliberately seeks temptation has already yielded to temptation, and in the effort to transcend childish ignorance has shown himself to be in the worst sense of the word a child and a dupe. 'Lead us not into temptation' – that petition in the prayer that our Lord taught His disciples ought to be the prayer of every strong Christian man, and I think it is correct to say that the stronger and the more mature a Christian man is, so much the more fervently will he pray that prayer.

It is very different, however, when temptation comes through no volition of our own – when we hate it and yet it comes. In those cases it may be the occasion for the attainment of new heights of victory. 'Count it all joy when ye fall into divers temptations' says the Epistle of James;[1] and if it be preferred to translate the word that is used there 'trials' instead of 'temptations' and to interpret it of persecutions which came to the Christians in that early age, still the meaning of the verse is not essentially different. If 'trials' are in view, rather than what we customarily call temptations, still those trials are here distinctly envisaged as involving temptations – temptations to discouragement, temptations to disloyalty to Christ, or the like. At any rate James here uses exactly the same Greek word to designate trials or temptations as that which is used in the petition in the Lord's Prayer as reported in the Gospel according to Matthew.

So our Lord taught us to pray, 'Lead us not into temptation';[2] yet the inspired writer of the Epistle of James bids us count it all joy when we fall into temptations. Is there any contradiction? No, there is not a bit of contradiction. It is very wicked to seek temptation; yet when it comes it may be a means of blessing, if God gives us strength to resist. It would be very wicked, for example, to pray for that kind of temptation which comes to a Christian through persecution from the adversaries of the faith; it would be

[1] James 1:2.   [2] Matt. 6:13.

THE CHRISTIAN VIEW OF MAN

very wicked to pray to God: 'O Lord, put it into the heart of this tyrannical ruler or that to persecute the Church, withdraw from him the restraints of Thy common grace, in order that the Church may receive the blessing which persecution might bring.' It would be very wrong to pray that prayer, and it would be very wrong to provoke a wicked ruler in any way whatever to persecuting zeal. Yet when persecution does come – does come, despite the prayers of God's people and despite their peaceable lives – it does remain true very often that 'the blood of the martyrs is the seed of the Church'. God over-rules evil for good.

So it is also with temptations in our own individual lives. It is very wrong to seek them; if we seek them we have already yielded to them in part. We ought resolutely to turn our eyes from things that are evil, and obey rather the Apostle's injunction: 'Finally, brethren, whatsoever things are true, whatsoever things are honest, whatsoever things are just, whatsoever things are pure, whatsoever things are lovely, whatsoever things are of good report; if there be any virtue, and if there be any praise, think on these things.'[1] Yet if temptations do come, and if we can honestly say in the secret of our own souls and in the presence of God who searches the heart that we have not sought them out but have prayed earnestly that they may be kept from us, then, if God gives us grace to resist, the temptations may be to us the means for the attainment of new strength and new power.

No, there is no contradiction whatever between the Lord's Prayer and the Epistle of James. The man who prays with all his soul, 'Lead us not into temptation,' will be just the man who will count it all joy when he falls into divers temptations and when he has the privilege of suf-

[1] Phil. 4:8

fering dishonour and pain at the hands of wicked men for the sake of his Lord.

Much that I have just said can be applied to the temptation that is narrated in the third chapter of Genesis. There are, it is true, important differences. The situation of Adam in the garden of Eden was different in important respects from the situation of the men who have lived after the fall. It was obviously different from the situation of those who have not believed in Jesus Christ for the salvation of their souls; for whereas Adam before the fall was good, those men are the slaves of sin. But it was also different from the situation of those who have been begotten anew by the power of the Holy Spirit and have been redeemed by the precious blood of Christ. No, never again will there be a return to the situation in which Adam found himself before the fall. That situation came once and once only in the whole history of mankind.

Yet there are certain fundamental principles of temptation which show themselves both in the Christian's present battle against sin and in the probation in which Adam stood according to the early chapters of the Book of Genesis. In both cases it does remain true, in accordance with the teaching of the Word of God, that temptation resisted brings advance for the soul of man.

What would have been the advance which resistance to that first temptation would have brought to Adam and Eve?

We have already pointed out the central feature of that advance. It would have meant, we have observed, that the possibility of sinning would have been over. The probation would successfully have been sustained; man would have entered into a blessedness from which all jeopardy would have been removed.

THE CHRISTIAN VIEW OF MAN

But the advance which a successful resistance to the temptation would have brought would also have been an advance in knowledge. That tree was called the tree of the knowledge of good and evil. Well, there is perhaps a real sense in which it would have been to man a tree of the knowledge of good and evil even if he had not eaten of the fruit of it. If he had resisted the temptation to eat of the fruit of that tree, he would have come to know evil in addition to the knowledge that he already had of good. He would not have known it because he had fallen into it in his own life, but he would have known it because in his resistance to it he would have put it sharply in contrast with good and would deliberately have rejected it. A state of innocence, in other words, where good was practised without any conflict with evil, would have given place to a state of assured goodness which evil would have been shown to have no power to disturb.

Such was the blessed state into which God was asking man to come when He entered into that covenant of life with him about which we spoke in the last of these talks. It was a state which included what I think we can call a knowledge of good and evil. Certainly it was a state in which the difference between good and evil would have been clearly discerned.

Such discernment was promised by the tempter. 'Ye shall be as God, knowing good and evil,' he said. But there was a right way and a wrong way of seeking to attain that discernment. The right way was the way of resistance to evil; the wrong way was the way of yielding to it and seeking to know it by experience.

How often that wrong way is suggested to men in the temptations that come to them now! Innocence being despised, the ancient lie is put into men's hearts again and again and again that the only way to attain a state higher than innocence is to have experience of sin in order to see what sin is like. Sowing wild oats is thought to be rather a good way of transcending childish innocence and of attaining strong and mature manhood.

Do you know how that lie can best be shown to be the lie that it is? Well, my friends, I think it is by the example of Jesus Christ. Do you despise innocence? Do you think that it is weak and childish not to have personal experience of evil? Do you think that if you do not obtain such experience of evil you must forever be a child?

If you have any such feeling, I just bid you contemplate Jesus of Nazareth. Does He make upon you any impression of immaturity or childishness? Was He lacking in some experience that is necessary to the highest manhood? Can you patronize Him as though He were but a child, whereas you with your boasted experience of evil are a full-grown man?

If that is the way you think of Jesus, even unbelievers, if they are at all thoughtful, will correct you. No, Jesus makes upon all thoughtful persons the impression of complete maturity and of tremendous strength. With unblinking eyes He contemplates the evil of the human heart. 'He knew what was in man,' says the Gospel according to John.[1] Yet He never had those experiences of sin which fools think to be necessary if innocence is to be transcended and the highest manhood is to be attained. From His spotless purity and His all-conquering strength, that ancient lie that experience of evil is necessary if man is to attain the highest good recoils naked and ashamed.

That was the lie that the tempter brought to Adam and

[1] John 2:25.

Eve in the garden of Eden. Man was told to seek discernment in Satan's way and not in God's.

Had man resisted the temptation what heights of knowledge and strength would have been his! Satan would have fled from him like a cringing slave and he would have entered forever into a state of kingship in company with God.

But he yielded, and what was the result? A sad result indeed! He sought to attain knowledge, and lost the knowledge of good; he sought to attain power, and lost his own soul; he sought to become as God, and when God came to him in the garden he hid himself in shameful fear.

It is a sad story indeed. But it is the beginning and not the end of the Bible. The first chapters of the Bible tell us of the sin of man. The guilt of that sin has rested upon every single one of us, its guilt and its terrible results; but that is not the last word of the Bible. The Bible tells us not only of man's sin; it also tells us of something greater still; it tells us of the grace of the offended God.

15: What is Sin?

WE COME NOW TO A VERY MOMENTOUS QUESTION
– the question 'What is sin?' We have spoken about the
first sin of man. Now we ask what sin at bottom is.

Widely different answers have been given to this question, and with these different answers have gone different
views of the world and of God and of human life.

The true answer is to be obtained, as we shall see, very
clearly in the Bible; but before I present that true answer
to you, I want to speak to you about one or two wrong
answers, in order that by contrast with them the true
answer may be the more clearly understood.

In the first place, many men have notions of sin which
really deprive sin of all its distinctiveness, or, rather, many
men simply deny the existence of anything that can properly be called sin at all.

According to a very widespread way of thinking in the
unbelief of the present day, what we popularly call morality is simply the accumulated experience of the race as to
the kind of conduct that leads to racial preservation and
well-being. Tribes in which every man sought his own
pleasure without regard to the welfare of his neighbours
failed, it is said, in the struggle for existence, whereas those
tribes that restrained the impulses of their members for the
good of the whole prospered and multiplied. By a process
of natural selection, therefore, according to this theory, it
came more and more to be true that among the races of
mankind those that cultivated solidarity were the ones that
survived.

In the course of time – so the theory runs – the lowly origin of these social restraints was altogether lost from view, and they were felt to be rooted in something distinctive that came to be called morality or virtue. It is only in modern times that we have got behind the scenes and have discovered the ultimate identity between what we call 'morality' and the self-interest of society.

Such is a very widespread theory. According to that theory 'sin' is only another name – and a very unsatisfactory name too – for anti-social conduct.

What shall we say of that notion of sin from the Christian point of view? The answer is surely quite plain. We must reject it very emphatically. 'Against thee, thee only, have I sinned,' says the Psalmist.[1] That is at the very heart of the Bible from beginning to end. Sin, according to the Bible, is not just conduct that is contrary to the accumulated experience of the race; it is not just anti-social conduct: but it is an offence primarily against God.

Equally destructive of any true idea of sin is the error of those who say that the end of all human conduct is, or (as some of them say) ought to be, pleasure.

Sometimes the pleasure which is regarded as the goal to be set before man is the pleasure of the individual – refined and thoroughly respectable pleasure no doubt, but still pleasure. Such a view has sometimes produced lives superficially decent. But even such superficial decency is not apt to be very lasting, and the degrading character of the philosophy underlying it is certain to make itself felt even on the surface sooner or later. Certainly that philosophy can never have a place for any notion that with any propriety at all could be called a true notion of sin.

Sometimes, it is true, the pleasure which is made the goal

[1] Ps. 51:4.

of human conduct is thought of as the pleasure, or (to use a more high-sounding word) the happiness, not of the individual but of the race. According to that view, altruism – namely, regard for the greatest happiness of the greatest number – is thought to be the sum-total of morality.

A little reflection will show how widespread and how influential this doctrine is. Examine, for example, some of the schemes of character-education which are being proposed for use in public schools or elsewhere. What do they amount to? Well, I am afraid they amount to an appeal to human experience as the basis of morality. This is the kind of conduct, they say in effect, which is found to work well; this is the kind of conduct, therefore, which good citizens ought to practise.

What should the Christian say of such schemes of so-called character-education? Well, I think he ought to oppose them with all his might. Far from building character they undermine character in the long run, because they substitute human experience, as the basis of morality, for the law of God.

The things that they advocate in detail are, indeed, in many cases things that the Christian man also can advocate. Certainly the notion that the greatest happiness of the greatest number is the thing that should be put before us as the goal does produce in detail many maxims of conduct that coincide with what the Christian, on his very different basis, advocates. It is obvious that murder and theft and robbery are not conducive to the greatest happiness of the greatest number, and it is also obvious that they are contrary to the Christian's standard. Therefore the Christian and the non-Christian, though for very different reasons, can unite in telling people not to enter upon a life of crime.

Nevertheless, the difference between Christian morality

and the morality of the world is a very important difference indeed.

For one thing, it is a difference even in details. Although there is a large area where the conduct advocated by modern utilitarians, on the basis of their principle that the standard of morality is to be found in the experience of the race, is exactly the same, in detail, as the conduct which is advocated by Christians, yet there are cases where the underlying difference of principle comes to the surface even in differences in detail.

Thus we have seen in the newspapers recently a good deal of discussion about 'mercy-killing' or 'euthanasia'. Certain physicians say very frankly that they think hopeless invalids, who never by any chance can be of use either to themselves or to anyone else, ought to be put painlessly out of the way. Are they right?

Well, I dare say a fairly plausible case might be made out for them on the basis of utilitarian ethics.

I am not quite sure – let me say in passing – that even on that basis it is a good case. This is a very dangerous business – this business of letting experts determine exactly what people 'never will be missed'. For my part, I do not believe in the infallibility of experts, and I think the tyranny of experts is the worst and most dangerous tyranny that ever was devised.

But, you see, that does not touch the real point. The real point is that the modern advocates of euthanasia are arguing the thing out on an entirely different basis from the basis on which the Christian argues it. They are arguing the question on the basis of what is useful – what produces happiness and avoids pain for the human race. The Christian argues it on the basis of a definite divine command. 'Thou shalt not kill' settles the matter for the Christian.

[176]

From the Christian point of view the physician who engages in a mercy-killing is just a murderer. It may also turn out that his mercy-killing is not really merciful in the long run. But that is not the point. The real point is that be it never so merciful, it is murder, and murder is sin.

The views of sin that we have considered so far are obviously opposed to Christianity. No Christian can hold that morality is just the accumulated self-interest of the race, and that sin is merely conduct opposed to such self-interest. The Christian obviously must hold that righteousness is something quite distinct from happiness and that sin is something quite distinct from folly.

Other erroneous views of sin, however, are not so obviously erroneous, and not so obviously, even though just as truly, anti-Christian.

There is, for example, the notion that sin is the triumph of the lower part of man's nature over the higher part, that it is the triumph of the appetites of the body over the human spirit – the human spirit which ought to be that in man which rules.

This definition appeals – falsely, it is true – to certain Biblical expressions, and it is a very ancient notion in the visible Christian Church.

In its extreme form, it represents matter as being in itself evil. The human soul or spirit is enclosed, it holds, in the prison house of the material world, and the goal of the soul's efforts should be to get free. Sin is everything that prevents that liberation of the soul from the material world.

Obviously such a doctrine is quite contrary to the Bible. It is a pagan notion, not a Christian notion. For one thing it really does away with the Christian idea of God altogether. If matter is essentially evil, and if God is good, then God could not have created matter, but matter must have existed always independently of Him. So it is not surprising to find that in the days of the ancient Church those who regarded matter as being essentially evil were dualists, not theists. That is, they did not believe in one God, creator of all things that exist, but they believed that there are two ultimately independent principles – a good principle, God; and an evil principle, matter.

In marked contrast with all such views, the Bible teaches from beginning to end that the material world, like the world of spirits, was created by God, and that none of God's works is to be regarded as evil.

Moreover, the Bible not only combats that view as a theory of the universe, but it also combats very earnestly the effects of it in human conduct. Those who regard matter as being essentially evil tend always to asceticism. They tend, always, that is, to abstention from enjoyment of the good things of this world as though such abstention were in itself a virtue – not a means to an end, but an end in itself; not a thing necessary on occasion, but a thing always necessary if real sainthood is to be attained.

To such asceticism the Bible is everywhere opposed. 'Touch not, taste not, handle not,' said the ascetics who were impairing the supremacy of Christ in the Colossian Church.[1] Very vigorously does the Apostle Paul combat their teaching. 'The earth is the Lord's, and the fulness thereof,' he says also in another Epistle.[2] So teaches the Bible from beginning to end. There is not a bit of support in Holy Scripture for the notion that the material world is essentially evil and that the enjoyment of it is sin.

At this point, however, there may possibly be an objection. Does not the Bible repeatedly designate 'the flesh' as an evil thing, and in doing so does it not teach that sin

[1] Col. 2:21. [2] I Cor. 10:26, 28.

consists after all in the triumph of man's lower or bodily nature over his higher nature?

To that objection we answer that certainly the Bible does repeatedly designate 'the flesh' as an evil thing, but that the whole question is what is meant in those passages by 'the flesh'?

Some people think that the word refers, in those passages, to the bodily nature of man, a lower part of his nature as over against a higher part. That view is presented in several of the recent translations of the Bible – better called mistranslations – which are leading so many people astray at the present time. One of those translations renders the word meaning 'the flesh' in the eighth chapter of Romans as 'the physical nature'; another translates it as 'the animal nature'.

Do you see exactly where those translations lead? They lead to the view that the conflict between the flesh and the Spirit according to the Epistles of Paul is a conflict between the physical and the spiritual part of man's nature, and that the triumph of the physical or animal nature in the conflict is what the Bible calls sin.

Is that view right? No, my friends, it is not right. On the contrary, it is a very deadly and far-reaching error. A man who holds that notion of sin has not the slightest inkling of what the Bible holds sin to be, and he is not apt, alas, to have the slightest inkling of what the Bible says about salvation from sin.

It is perfectly true, of course, that in many places the Bible means by 'flesh' simply a certain part of the bodily structure of man or animals. It speaks of 'flesh and blood' or the like. That is the simple, physical sense of the word. Undoubtedly it does occur in the Bible.

But we are speaking now about those passages where

'the flesh' is presented in the Bible as an evil thing. Does the word have its simple, physical meaning in those passages?

The answer is emphatically, 'No'. In those passages the word is used in a very special sense indeed – a sense far removed from the original, purely physical sense. In those passages it designates not the physical nature of man or the animal nature of man, but the whole nature of man, as that nature is now, in its fallen condition, separate from God.

The principal stages by which the word 'flesh' comes to have that meaning in the Bible seem to be fairly clear. First, the simple physical meaning. Then 'flesh' designating man in his weakness, all of him being designated by a word that properly designates the part of him in which his weakness is most clearly shown, as when the Bible says: 'All flesh is grass, and all the goodliness thereof is as the flower of the field.'[1] Then 'flesh' designating man as he now is, lost in sin – as he now is until he is transformed by the Spirit of God. It is this third meaning of the word which is found in those great passages where 'the flesh' is represented in the Bible as being an evil thing.

As thus used, the word does not designate a lower part of man's nature as over against a higher part. It designates all of man's nature, in its present sinful state, as over against the divine holiness. It does not designate the body of man as over against the spirit of man, but it designates the whole of man as over against the Spirit of God.

That appears with particular clearness in such a passage as I Cor. 3:3, where Paul says: 'For ye are yet carnal: for whereas there is among you envying, and strife, and divisions, are ye not carnal, and walk as men?' The word translated 'carnal' here comes from the word for flesh; it

[1] Isa. 40:6.

might just as well be translated 'fleshly'. Well, what does it mean? The Apostle tells us himself. 'Are ye not carnal, and walk as men?' he says. Evidently being carnal or fleshly and walking as men are intended here to be taken as the same thing. One of these expressions explains the other. How ought the Corinthian Christians to walk? According to God. How do they actually walk? According to men. But walking according to men as distinguished from walking according to God is, Paul says, the same as being fleshly. Thus the flesh does not mean, as those sadly mistaken translations of the Bible make it mean, the animal nature of man as distinguished from some higher part of his nature; it means simply all of human nature – that is, human nature as it now is, under the control of sin, as distinguished from the Spirit of God.

Paul makes the thing even clearer in the following verse, according to the text of the best manuscripts which is rightly followed in the Revised Version: 'For when one saith, I am of Paul; and another, I am of Apollos; are ye not men?' Here the Apostle treats being men – that is, being merely men, and not transformed by the Spirit of God – actually as a thing worthy of blame and as just the same thing as being fleshly. 'Are ye not fleshly?' he says in the preceding verse. 'Are ye not men?' he says in this verse. The two mean the same thing, and they both mean being controlled or acting as though one were controlled simply by one's fallen human nature as distinguished from being controlled by the Spirit of God.

What a gulf there is between this Biblical way of regarding fallen human nature and the modern paganism, proclaimed by so many preachers of the present day, which actually takes as a leading article in its creed the words, 'I believe in man'. What a gulf there is between the modern

THE CHRISTIAN VIEW OF MAN

pagan confidence in human resources and the teaching of
the Bible, which makes the question, 'Are ye not men?' the
same thing as 'Are ye not carnal?' and treats both questions as bringing a terrible reproach to Christian people!

Thus sin, according to the Bible, is not just 'the brute in
us'. No, it is very much more serious than that. Alas, sin
is not the brute in us; it is, rather, the man in us. It is the
man in us, because the whole man, spirit or soul just as
much as body, is sold under sin, until transformed by the
regenerating power of the Spirit of God.

Certainly the Bible does teach that sin sits in our bodies,
that it makes our bodies its instruments, and that uncon-
trolled bodily appetites constitute a very large part of the
occasion for our falling. All that is perfectly true. But that
is very different indeed from saying that bodily appetites
constitute the essence of sin. No, when the Bible gives us
one of those terrible lists of sins that occur, for example,
here and there in the Epistles of Paul, when it catalogues,
as in the fifth chapter of Galatians, 'the works of the
flesh',[1] it includes not only what we are accustomed to
speak of as fleshly sins but also, and very prominently,
sins such as pride and hatred, which are not in our sense
sins of the flesh at all. Indeed those sins of pride and the
like, and not what we call fleshly sins, are just the sins that
Paul is speaking of in that passage in I Corinthians when
he charges his readers with being fleshly.

The Bible finds sin, moreover, in a world of spirits – it
speaks of spiritual hosts of wickedness in high places[2] –
as it finds sin, alas, in the spirit of fallen man. If we want
to be true to the Bible, we must get rid of this whole notion
that the essence of sin is found in the rebellion of a lower
part of our nature against a higher part.

[1] Gal. 5:19–21.   [2] Eph. 6:12.

What, then, is sin? We have said what it is not. Now we ought to say what it is.

Fortunately we do not have to search very long in the Bible to find the answer to that question. The Bible gives the answer right at the beginning in the account that it gives of the very first sin of man – that account which we studied together in the previous one of these little talks.

What was that first sin of man, according to the Bible? Was it the gratification of a bodily appetite? Yes, it was that. The woman saw that the tree was good for food and that it was pleasant to the eyes, we are told. But was the sin merely the gratification of a bodily appetite? Most certainly not! No, it was a highly intellectual, spiritual thing. The serpent said that the eating of the fruit of that tree would make man wise. That part of it was not a bodily appetite at all.

What, then, was that first sin of man? Is not the answer perfectly clear? Why, it was disobedience to a command of God. God said, 'Ye shall not eat of the fruit of the tree'; man ate of the fruit of the tree: and that was sin. There we have our definition of sin at last.

'Sin is any want of conformity unto, or transgression of, the law of God.' Those are the words of the Shorter Catechism, not of the Bible; but they are true to what the Bible teaches from Genesis to Revelation.

16: The Majesty of the Law of God

IN THE LAST OF THESE TALKS WE CONSIDERED THE momentous question, 'What is sin?' Various answers to that question have been given, but the true answer, we observed, is the one that is contained in the Shorter Catechism. 'Sin,' the Shorter Catechism says, 'is any want of conformity unto, or transgression of, the law of God.'

The full meaning of that definition will become clearer, I hope, as we go on to speak of the consequences of Adam's sin for the human race.

Just now, however, we are taking the thing only in its simplest and most obvious form. The most elementary thing about sin is that it is that which is contrary to God's law. You cannot believe in the existence of sin unless you believe in the existence of the law of God. The idea of sin and the idea of law go together. Think of sin, in the Biblical sense of the word, and you think of law; think of law, and – at least as humanity now is – you think of sin.

That being so, I ask you just to run through the Bible in your mind and consider how very pervasive in the Bible is the Bible's teaching about the law of God.

We have already observed how clear that teaching is in the account which the Bible gives of the first sin of man. God said, 'Ye shall not eat of the fruit of the tree'. That was God's law; it was a definite command. Man disobeyed that command; man did what God told him not to do: and that was sin.

But the law of God runs all through the Bible. It is not found just in this passage or that, but it is the background of everything that the Bible says regarding the relations between God and man.

Consider for a moment how large a part of the Old Testament is occupied with the law of God – the law as it was given through Moses. Do you think that came by chance? Not at all. It came because the law is truly fundamental in what the Bible has to say.

All through the Old Testament there is held up a great central thought – God the lawgiver, man owing obedience to Him.

How is it, then, with the New Testament? Does the New Testament obscure that thought; does the New Testament depreciate in any way the law of God?

There have been those who have thought so. The error called 'antinomianism' has held that the dispensation of grace which was ushered in by Christ abrogated the law of God for Christian people.

What a truly horrible error that is! It is certainly true, in one sense, that Christians are, as Paul says, not under the law but under grace. They are not subject to the curse which the law pronounces against sin; Christ has set them free from that curse by bearing the curse in their stead on the Cross. They are not under any dispensation where their acceptance with God depends upon their own obedience to God's law; instead, their acceptance with God depends upon the obedience which Christ accomplished for them. All that is perfectly true. But does that mean that for Christian people the law of God is no longer the expression of God's will which they are solemnly obligated to obey; does it mean that they are now free to do as they please and are no longer bound by God's commands?

Let the whole Bible, let the whole New Testament, in particular, give the answer.

THE CHRISTIAN VIEW OF MAN

'Think not,' said Jesus, 'that I am come to destroy the law, or the prophets: I am not come to destroy, but to fulfil.'[1] Then He goes on to place His righteousness in contrast with the righteousness of the scribes and Pharisees. Is it easier than theirs? No, He Himself tells us that it is harder. 'For I say unto you,' He says, 'that except your righteousness shall exceed the righteousness of the scribes and Pharisees, ye shall in no case enter into the kingdom of heaven.' Does His righteousness partake less of the nature of law than the rules which the scribes and Pharisees set up? Is His righteousness something that a man can take with a grain of salt; is it something that he can suit himself about heeding? Well, I can only say, my friends, that if that is the way you read the words of Jesus as they are recorded in the Gospels, you have not even got barely to the threshold of understanding them. 'And if thy right eye offend thee,' says Jesus, 'pluck it out, and cast it from thee: for it is profitable for thee that one of thy members should perish, and not that thy whole body should be cast into hell.'[2] 'But I say unto you,' He says in another place, 'that every idle word that men shall speak, they shall give account thereof in the day of judgment.'[3] Are these the words of one who substitutes some other reign for the reign of the law of God? Are these the words of one who believed that men could trifle with God's law?

I know that some people hold – by a veritable delirium of folly, as it seems to me – that the words of Jesus belong to a dispensation of law that was brought to a close by His death and resurrection and that therefore the teaching of the Sermon on the Mount, for example, is not intended for the dispensation of grace in which we are now living.

Well, let them turn to the Apostle Paul, the Apostle who

[1] Matt. 5:17.   [2] Matt. 5:29.   [3] Matt. 12:36.

has told us that we are not under the law but under grace. What does he say about the matter? Does he represent the law of God as a thing without validity in this dispensation of divine grace?

Not at all. In the second chapter of Romans, as well as (by implication) everywhere else in his Epistles, he insists upon the universality of the law of God. Even the Gentiles, though they do not know that clear manifestation of God's law which was found in the Old Testament, have God's law written upon their hearts and are without excuse when they disobey. Christians, in particular, Paul insists, are far indeed from being emancipated from the duty of obedience to God's commands. The Apostle regards any such notion as the deadliest of errors. 'Now the works of the flesh,' says Paul, 'are manifest, which are these: Adultery, fornication, uncleanness, lasciviousness, idolatry, witchcraft, hatred, variance, emulations, wrath, strife, seditions, heresies, envyings, murders, drunkenness, revellings, and such like: of the which I tell you before, as I have also told you in time past, that they which do such things shall not inherit the kingdom of God.'[1]

Great, indeed, according to Paul, is the advantage of the Christian, as of those who even before Christ came were saved by the merit of the sacrifice that He was to make upon the Cross (being saved, as Christians are now, by the grace of God through faith). Christians are not under the curse of the law; in that tremendous sense they are not under the law but under grace. Christ has borne the just penalty of the law for them. They have moreover within them a new power, the power of the Holy Spirit, which the law of itself could never give.

But that new power does not emancipate them from obe-

[1] Gal. 5:19-21.

dience to God's holy commands. Nay, it enables them to obey those commands as they could never obey them before.

Consider for a moment, my friends, the majesty of the law of God as the Bible sets it forth. One law over all – valid for Christians, valid for non-Christians, valid now and valid to all eternity. How grandly that law is promulgated amid the thunderings of Sinai! How much more grandly still and much more terribly it is set forth in the teaching of Jesus – in His teaching and in His example! With what terror we are fain to say, with Peter, in the presence of that dazzling purity: 'Depart from me; for I am a sinful man, O Lord.'[1] Nowhere in the Bible, in the teaching of Jesus our Saviour, do we escape from the awful majesty of the law of God – written in the constitution of the universe, searching the innermost recesses of the soul, embracing every idle word and every action and every secret thought of the heart, inescapable, all-inclusive, holy, terrible. God the lawgiver, man the subject; God the ruler, man the ruled! The service of God is a service that is perfect freedom, a duty that is the highest of all joys; yet it is a service still. Let us never forget that. God was always and is forever the sovereign King; the whole universe is beneath His holy law.

That is the atmosphere in which the Bible moves; that is the rock upon which it is founded. God's law embracing all! And what sort of law is that? Is it an arbitrary enactment of some cruel tyrant, a meaningless sport of one whose power exceeds His wisdom or His goodness? No, this law is grounded in the infinite perfection of the being of God Himself. 'Be ye therefore perfect,' said Jesus, 'even as your Father which is in heaven is perfect.'[2] That is the

[1] Lk. 5:8. [2] Matt. 5:48.

standard. God's law is no arbitrary or meaningless law; it is a holy law, as God Himself is holy.

If that be the law of God, how awful a thing is sin! What tongue can tell the horror of it? Not an offence against some temporary or arbitrary rule proceeding from temporal authority or enforced by temporal penalties, but an offence against the infinite and eternal God! What nameless terror steals over us when we really contemplate such guilt as that!

But do we really contemplate it? That question must certainly be asked. I know that some of my hearers regard what I have been saying as being no more worthy of consideration than the hobgoblins and bogies with which nurses used to frighten naughty children. An outstanding characteristic of the age in which we are living is a disbelief in anything that can be called a law of God and in particular a disbelief in anything that can properly be called sin. The plain fact is that the men of our day are living for the most part in an entirely different world of thought and feeling and life from the world in which the Christian lives. The difference does not just concern this detail or that: it concerns the entire basis of life; it concerns the entire atmosphere in which men live and move and have their being. At the heart of everything that the Bible says are two great truths, which belong inseparably together – the majesty of the law of God, and sin as an offence against that law. Both these basic truths are denied in modern society, and in the denial of them is found the central characteristic of the age in which we are living.

Well, what sort of age is that; what sort of age is this in which the law of God is regarded as obsolete and in which there is no consciousness of sin?

I will tell you. It is an age in which the disintegration of society is proceeding on a gigantic scale. Look about you, and what do you see? Everywhere the throwing off of restraint, the abandonment of standards, the return to barbarism.

But, you say, has not liberty at least been attained? Now that morality has been abandoned – Victorian convention and all that – surely liberty must have free course. Ah, but does it, my friends? A man has to be completely blind to say that it does. On the contrary, liberty lies prostrate in Russia, in Germany, in Italy and in many other countries of the earth. How slow was the progress of Europe up from tyranny to democracy and freedom! And now that hard-won liberty is rapidly being thrown away.

There are indeed islands of resistance to the tyrant's march. We read the other day how the people of Great Britain stood silent when they received the news that their king – symbol of liberty! – had died. A hush seemed to fall upon the nation, and selfish strife for the moment ceased. It was an eloquent silence indeed – eloquent of the love of a great people for things that treasure can never buy, eloquent of centuries of glorious history.

'This happy breed of men, this little world,
This precious stone set in the silver sea,
Which serves it in the office of a wall,
Or as a moat defensive to a house,
Against the envy of less happier lands, –
This blessed plot, this earth, this realm, this England.'

But do you think that even Great Britain is safe – safe, I mean, not from the battleships and the airplanes and the armies of her enemies, but safe from the far more dangerous foes within?

I do not think so, my friends. Safe, no doubt, if any

country of the earth is safe; but still not safe. Look back upon the history of Great Britain, and I think you will see that always before she had one possession that she is now in danger of losing. She had the conviction that there is a transcendent principle of right to which all the peoples of the world are subject. I know that there were times when that eternal principle of right was lost very largely from view. There were times of widespread debauchery. There have been times in the history of the British Empire when some very terrible national crimes were committed. But always there was a large remnant in the British people that had a firm and well-grounded belief in their obligation to the law of God. That was the precious salt that preserved the nation from decay, and gave it that marvellous stability which ought to be an object of emulation to the whole civilized world. Liberty under the law of God – that and not far-flung battle lines or an Empire upon which the sun never sets – is the thing that has made Great Britain great.

Today that is seriously endangered in Great Britain as well as everywhere else. There too there are hosts of people who do not believe that there is a law of God, and the number of those who do believe it is smaller today, and is less influential in the heart of the national life, than it has ever been in recent centuries. I do not know whether you agree with me, my friends, but I am bound to say that I am afraid for Great Britain today, and being afraid even for Great Britain I am still more afraid for all the rest of the world. Everywhere tyranny is stalking through the earth, and decadence disguised under a hundred new-fangled and high-sounding names.

Well, what shall be done about it? Many people not Christians at all agree with us in holding that something ought to be done. Even materialists and other atheists can see that. Something obviously has to be done even to keep the animal, man, in some kind of healthy condition upon the earth – to prevent him from destroying himself, for example, by another world war.

So all sorts of things are being proposed to check the ravages of crime. One proposes that we shall all be finger-printed and be treated like paroled criminals required to show identification cards as we walk the streets, whenever required to do so according to the whims of the police, – no longer allowed to go about our business unhindered until there is some sort of legitimate suspicion that we are guilty of crime. Another proposes that teachers even in private schools and Christian schools shall be regarded as government officials, being required to take an oath of allegiance as is done in Hitlerized Germany. A thousand nostrums are being brought to our attention, different in many particulars but all alike in being destructive of that civil and religious liberty which our fathers won at such cost.

Such measures will never accomplish even the end that they have in view. Patriotism can never be implanted in people's hearts by force. The attempt to do that serves only to crush out patriotism when it is already there. The march of communism or other forms of slavery can never be checked by suppression of freedom of speech. Such suppression serves only to render more dangerous the progress of the destructive ideas.

What then is the remedy for the threatened disruption of society and for the rapidly progressing decay of liberty?

There is really only one remedy. It is the rediscovery of the law of God.

If we want to restore respect for human laws, we shall

have to get rid of this notion that judges and juries exist only for the utilitarian purpose of the protection of society, and shall have to restore the notion that they exist for the purposes of justice. They are only very imperfect exponents of justice, it is true. There are vast departments of life with which they should have nothing whatever to do. They are exceeding their God-given function when they seek to enforce inward purity or purity of the individual life, since theirs is the business only of enforcing – and that in necessarily imperfect fashion – that part of righteousness which concerns the relations between man and man. But they are instruments of righteousness all the same, and when that is not recognized, disaster follows for the state. Society will never be preserved by attaching savage penalties to trifling offences because the utilitarian interests of society demand it; it will never be preserved by the vicious practice (followed by some judges) of making 'examples' of people in spasmodic and unjust fashion because such examples are thought to have a salutary effect as a deterrent from future crime. No, we say, let justice never be lost from view – abstract, holy, transcendent justice – no matter what the immediate consequences may be thought to be. Only so will the ermine of the judge again be respected and the ravages of decadence be checked.

Ah, but all that does not touch the really important matter. Underlying all these considerations of nations and of society is the great question of the relation of the soul to God. Unless men are right with God, they will never be right in their relations with one another.

How, then, shall they be right with God? Oh, you say, there is the gospel; there is the sweet and comforting teaching of Jesus Christ.

Yes, but do men come to Jesus Christ? Do they come to Him for the salvation of their souls? No, they patronize Him as a fine religious teacher, and then they pass Him by.

How, then, shall they be brought to Him? The Bible gives the answer. 'Wherefore,' it says, 'the law was our schoolmaster to bring us unto Christ, that we might be justified by faith.'[1] That was true of the Hebrews in Old Testament and post-Old Testament times, about whom Paul is speaking in that passage; but it is also true of everyone who really and truly comes to Jesus Christ as his Saviour from sin. The consciousness of sin alone leads men to turn to the Saviour from sin, and the consciousness of sin comes only when men are brought face to face with the law of God.

But men have no consciousness of sin today, and what are we going to do? I remember that that problem was presented very poignantly in my hearing some time ago by a preacher who was sadly puzzled. Here we are, said he. We are living in the twentieth century. We have to take things as we find them; and as a matter of fact, whether we like it or not, if we talk to the young people of the present day about sin and guilt they will not know what we are talking about; they will simply turn away from us in utter boredom, and they will turn from the Christ whom we preach. Is not that really too bad? he continued. Is it not really too bad for them to miss the blessing that Christ has for them if only they would come to Him? If, therefore, they will not come to Christ in our way, ought we not to invite them to come in their way? If they will not come to Christ through the consciousness of sin induced by the terror of the law of God, may we not get them to come through the attraction of the amiable ethics of Jesus and

[1] Gal. 3:24.

the usefulness of His teaching in solving the problems of society?

I am afraid that in response to such questions we shall just have to answer, 'No'. I am afraid we shall just have to say that being a Christian is a much more tragic thing than these people suppose. I am afraid we shall just have to tell them that they cannot clamber over the wall into the Christian way. I am afraid we shall just have to point them to the little wicket gate, and tell them to seek their Saviour while yet He may be found, in order that He may rescue them from the day of wrath.

But is not that utterly hopeless? Is it not utterly hopeless to try to get the people of the twentieth century to take the law of God with any seriousness or to be the slightest bit frightened about their sins?

I answer, Certainly it is hopeless. Absolutely hopeless. As hopeless as it is for a camel to try to pass through the eye of a needle.

But, you see, there is One who can do hopeless things. That is, the Spirit of the living God.

Do not fear, you Christians. The Spirit of God has not lost His power. In His own good time, He will send His messengers even to a wicked and adulterous and careless generation. He will cause Mount Sinai to overhang and shoot forth flames; He will convict men of sin; He will break down men's pride; He will melt their stony hearts. Then He will lead them to the Saviour of their souls.

17: Is Mankind Lost in Sin?

WE HAVE SPOKEN OF THE FIRST SIN OF MAN, AND we have spoken of the question, 'What is sin?' The question now arises what consequences that first sin of man has had for us and for all men.

Some people think it had very slight consequences – if indeed these people think that there ever was a first sin of man at all, in the sense in which it is described in the third chapter of Genesis.

I remember that some years ago, when I was driving home in my car after a summer vacation, I stayed over Sunday in a certain city without any particular reason except that I do not like to travel on that day. Being without any acquaintance with the city, I dropped into what seemed perhaps to be the leading church in the central part of the town.

What I heard in that church was typical of what one hears in a great many churches today. There was nothing particularly remarkable about it. I really do not know just why it has lingered so long in my memory, since I have of course heard essentially the same thing said in many places and in many ways.

It was the Sunday on which the new Sunday School teachers were being inducted into office. The pastor preached a sermon appropriate to the occasion. There are two notions about the teaching of children in the Church, he said. According to one notion, the children are to be told that they are sinners and need a Saviour. That is the old notion, he said; it has been abandoned in the modern Church. According to the other notion, he said, which is of course the notion that we moderns hold, the business of the teacher is to nurture the tender plant of the religious nature of the child in order that it may bear fruit in a normal and healthy religious life.

Was that preacher right, or was what he designated as the old notion right? Are children born good, or are they born bad? Do they need, in order that they may grow up into Christian manhood, merely the use of the resources planted in them at birth, or do they need a new birth and a divine Saviour?

That is certainly a momentous question. We may answer the question in this way or in that, but about the importance of the question I do not see how there can well be any doubt. That preacher, in the church of which I have spoken, recognized the importance of the question. That was why I was interested in his sermon. He answered the question that he raised quite wrongly, but at least he was right in looking the question fairly in the face.

In the present talk and the next one, I propose that we should imitate that preacher in facing the question fairly, even though our conclusion may turn out to be different from his. Are children born good or are they born bad? Is each man the captain of his own soul, and a pretty capable captain too, or is all mankind lost in sin?

How shall we answer the question? I see only one way. It is the way of simply asking what God has told us about it in His holy Word. Does the Bible teach that children are born into the world good (or at least evenly balanced between badness and goodness), or does it teach that all save one child are born in sin?

When we approach the Bible with that question in our

minds, one thing is at once perfectly clear. It is that the Bible from Genesis to Revelation teaches that all men (with the one exception of Jesus Christ) are as a matter of fact sinners in the sight of God. How they all came to be sinners is another question of which we shall speak in the following talk, but what we are now concerned to observe is that according to the Bible they are as a matter of fact all sinners.

In one great passage, particularly, that truth, that all men are sinners, is made the subject of definite exposition and proof. That passage is found in Romans 1:18–3:20. There the Apostle Paul, before he goes on to set forth the gospel, sets forth the universal need of the gospel. All have need of the gospel, he says, because all without exception are sinners. The Gentiles are sinners. They have disobeyed God's law, even though they have not that law in the particularly clear form in which it was presented to God's chosen people through Moses. Because they have disobeyed God's law, and as a punishment for their disobedience of it, they have sunk deeper and deeper into the mire of sin. The Jews also, says Paul, are sinners. They have great advantages; they have a special revelation from God; in particular they have a supernatural revelation of God's law. But it is not the hearing of the law that causes a man to be righteous but the doing of it; and the Jews, alas, though they have heard it, have not done it. They too are transgressors.

So all have sinned, according to Paul. He drives that truth home by a series of Old Testament Scripture quotations beginning with the words: 'There is none righteous, no, not one: there is none that understandeth, there is none that seeketh after God. They are all gone out of the way, they are together become unprofitable; there is none that doeth good, no, not one.'[1]

I think it is hardly too much to say that if this Pauline teaching about the universal sinfulness of mankind is untrue, the whole of the rest of that glorious Epistle, the Epistle to the Romans, falls to the ground. Imagine Paul as admitting that a single mere man since the fall ever was righteous in the sight of God, not needing, therefore, redemption through the precious blood of Christ; and you see at once that such a Paul would be a totally different Paul from the one who speaks in every page of the Epistle to the Romans and in every one of the other Pauline Epistles that the New Testament contains. The light of the gospel, in the teaching of Paul, stands out always against the dark background of a race universally lost in sin.

Is the case any different in the rest of the Bible? Well, we have not time here to pass all the sixty-six books of the Bible in review, but if you will just try to think of them as a whole as well as you can at this moment, you will see, I feel sure, that the universality of sin is at the very heart and core of the message that they contain. I care not at this point whether you turn to the Old Testament or to the New Testament. Everywhere there is the same terrible diagnosis of the ill of mankind. Brushing aside all excuses, the Bible teaches us everywhere to look at ourselves as God looks at us, and doing that it bids us beat upon our breasts and cry to God: 'Unclean, unclean!'

I know that some people hold that an exception is to be found in this gloomy chorus of the Biblical books. Paul, they admit, believed that all are sinners and need to have their sins washed away in a holy victim's blood, but Jesus,

[1] Rom. 3:10-12.

they say, appealed with confidence to the good that men's hearts contained.

Do you know, my friends, I am amazed when I hear people talk in that way. I am not amazed because they show thereby that they themselves have no consciousness of sin. Alas, the lack of a consciousness of sin is only too common among those whose hearts have never been touched by the Holy Spirit in saving grace. But what does amaze me is that educated men, living in the supposedly enlightened twentieth century, should show so little historical sense as to attribute their own pagan confidence in humanity to Jesus of Nazareth. I am not surprised that *they* have confidence in man, but I am considerably surprised that they should think that Jesus had.

Of course if they think so they must put the four Gospels aside, as those Gospels stand in the New Testament. That is clear at the start; for in the Fourth Gospel it is said in so many words that Jesus did not have confidence in man. 'Now when he was in Jerusalem,' the Fourth Gospel says, 'at the passover, in the feast day, many believed in his name, when they saw the miracles which he did. But Jesus did not commit himself unto them, because he knew all men, and needed not that any should testify of man: for he knew what was in man.'[1] Alas, Jesus knew what was in man only too well. Others, who looked merely upon the outward appearance, might have confidence in human goodness; but He knew the depths of the heart, and knowing those depths He was slow to trust those who seemed at least superficially to trust Him.

No doubt this passage does not mean that Jesus' estimate of all men was like His estimate of those who came to Him at that first passover time in Jerusalem. The meaning

[1] John 2: 23–25.

is rather that because of His profound insight into the human heart He could discriminate between those who were relatively trustworthy and those who were not; He did not need that anyone should tell him, 'Beware of this man or that,' but could Himself tell which men were not to be trusted.

All the same, the passage does give a picture of Jesus which is far removed indeed from the picture given by those who make Him an adherent of the modern creed, 'I believe in man'. This Jesus of the Fourth Gospel is no advocate of that incorrigible optimism regarding human nature which is thought to be a virtue by so many preachers of the present day.

Indeed, according to the Fourth Gospel, Jesus said to Nicodemus, 'Ye must be born again', and 'Except a man be born again, he cannot see the kingdom of God'.[1] All that men call goodness, in other words, is useless if a man would come into God's presence. He must receive a new birth if he would be received. The universal sinfulness of mankind is there taught with a plainness that could hardly be surpassed.

Of course the Fourth Gospel will not be accepted by the preachers of whom I am now speaking. Most of them will not admit that it was written by John the Apostle or that it gives a truthful account of what Jesus really taught.

How is it, then, with the other three Gospels? Do they give any other account of Jesus' attitude toward human claims to goodness than that which is given in the Gospel according to John?

No, they give exactly the same account. Let us look at this thing carefully and fairly.

Before Jesus began His public ministry, according to the

[1] John 3:3, 7.

three Synoptic Gospels, there had appeared a prophet called John the Baptist.

Well, what did this great prophet do? He called on the people to be baptized unto the remission of sins. So the people came to him confessing that they were sinners.

Did he call on some of the people to confess their sins and be baptized, or did he call upon all of them? This question needs only to be put, in order that it may be answered. Without a doubt he called on all of them – all save the one sinless man, Jesus of Nazareth. Surely that indicates, then, that he held them all, save that one, to be sinners.

Indeed, in this universal call to repentance John the Baptist did not even make exception of himself. 'I have need to be baptized of thee,' he said as Jesus came to him to be baptized, 'and comest thou to me?'[1] What a clear testimony that is to the universal sinfulness of mankind! Even John the Baptist was not exempt. He was a stern preacher of righteousness; he called the people to repentance. But before he called the people to repentance he repented himself. In the presence of the holiness of the Son of God, John the Baptist, greatest of the prophets, confessed himself a sinner like the rest.

Did Jesus differ from the teaching of John the Baptist at this point? John the Baptist taught the universal sinfulness of mankind. Did Jesus repudiate such teaching?

Surely that question, again, needs only to be asked in order that it may be answered. Far from repudiating John the Baptist's ministry, Jesus put the unmistakable stamp of His approval upon it. 'What went ye out into the wilderness to see?' He said. 'A reed shaken with the wind? . . . But what went ye out for to see? A prophet? Yea, I say

[1] Matt. 3:14.

unto you, and more than a prophet. . . . Verily I say unto you, Among them that are born of women there hath not risen a greater than John the Baptist. . . .'¹ Evidently Jesus regarded that stern preacher of righteousness as His true forerunner. The necessary preparation for Jesus' ministry was, according to Jesus Himself, the recognition of that universal sinfulness which John the Baptist so powerfully proclaimed.

We cannot, however, stop there. Jesus did not teach the universal sinfulness of mankind (and the consequent universal need of repentance) merely by endorsing the Baptist who taught these things. No, He also taught these things Himself. Do you remember how the Gospel according to Matthew reports the preaching with which Jesus came forward in Galilee after John the Baptist had been put into prison? Well, it reports it in exactly the same words as those in which it reports the Baptist's preaching. 'Repent,' said Jesus: 'for the kingdom of heaven is at hand.'² That is word for word what John the Baptist had said.³ Exactly like His forerunner, Jesus came forward with a call for repentance of sin.

Did Jesus address that call to all of the people or only to some? Did He say: 'Repent, those of you who are sinners, but there are some of you who need no repentance'?

There is one saying of Jesus in the Gospels which, if we took it absolutely alone, and closed our eyes completely to the connection in which it was spoken, might lead us to say that Jesus did make exceptions in His call to repentance. 'I came not,' He said, 'to call the righteous, but sinners to repentance.'⁴ Ah, but, my friends, when we take this verse in its context and in connection with all the

¹ Matt. 11: 7–11.　　² Matt. 4:17.　　³ Matt. 3:2.　　⁴ Mk. 2:17.

rest of Jesus' teaching, we see that those among Jesus' hearers who placed themselves in the category of the righteous who need no repentance were regarded by Jesus as needing repentance most of all.

'Two men,' said Jesus, 'went up into the temple to pray; the one a Pharisee, and the other a publican. The Pharisee stood and prayed thus with himself, God, I thank thee, that I am not as other men are, extortioners, unjust, adulterers, or even as this publican. I fast twice in the week, I give tithes of all that I possess. And the publican, standing afar off, would not lift up so much as his eyes unto heaven, but smote upon his breast, saying, God be merciful to me a sinner.'[1]

Which of those two men received a blessing from God when he prayed there in the temple – the man who thought he was an exception to God's call to repentance or the one who beat upon his breast and confessed himself a sinner? Jesus tells us very plainly. The publican went down to his house justified rather than the other.

Ah, my friends, how terrible is the rebuke of Jesus again and again and again for those who think that they form exceptions to the universal sinfulness of mankind!

A rich young ruler came running to Jesus one day, and asked him, 'Good Master, what shall I do that I may inherit eternal life?' Jesus repeated to him a number of the commandments. The man said, 'All these have I observed from my youth'. Jesus said: 'One thing thou lackest: go thy way, sell whatsoever thou hast, and give to the poor.' The young man went away sorrowful.[2]

Do you think that was a bad young man? No, he was a good young man – that is, if any man is good. We are expressly told that when Jesus looked at him He loved him.

[1] Lk. 18:10–13.   [2] Mk. 10:17–22.

Yet he lacked something; he was not good as God regards goodness.

I do not think the point of the narrative is found in the particular thing that he lacked. The point is rather that every man always lacks something. No man comes up to God's standard; no man can inherit the kingdom of God if he stands upon his own obedience to God's law.

Did you ever observe what incident comes just before this incident of the rich young ruler in all three of the Synoptic Gospels – in Matthew and in Mark and in Luke? It is the incident of the bringing of little children to Jesus, when Jesus said to the disciples, as reported in Mark and similarly in Luke: 'Whosoever shall not receive the kingdom of God as a little child, he shall not enter therein.'[1] There is a profound connection between these two incidents, as there is also a connection of both of them with the parable of the Pharisee and the Publican which in Luke immediately precedes.

Some years ago I heard a sermon on the incident of the Rich Young Ruler. I suppose that in the course of my life I have heard other sermons on that incident, but they have all gone completely from my memory. What are the sermons that we are apt to remember? I think they are the sermons where the preacher does not preach himself but where he truly unfolds the meaning of some great passage of the Word of God. After we have heard such a sermon, then when we come to that passage ever and again in our reading of the Bible, we think of the way in which God's messenger made the meaning of it clear to us; and we thank God anew.

The sermon of which I am now thinking is one which was preached some time ago in a Philadelphia church by

[1] Mk. 10:15.

my colleague, Professor R. B. Kuiper. He took the incident of the Rich Young Ruler together with the incident of the bringing of the little children to Jesus, and he showed how both incidents teach the same great lesson – the lesson of the utter helplessness of man the sinner and the absolute necessity of the free grace of God. You cannot depend for your entrance into the kingdom of God upon anything that you have or anything that you are. You must be poor, and you must be a child. You must be utterly poor in order that you may enter in, and you must be as helpless as a little child. Your reliance cannot be on your own goodness, for you have none. It can only be upon the mysterious grace of God.

I tell you, my friends, that teaching does not lie merely somewhere upon the surface of Jesus' teaching; it lies at the very heart of it. The great central message of Jesus Christ – nay, also His great central work in the gift of Himself for sinners upon the Cross – is altogether without meaning unless all men without exception are sinners deserving only God's wrath and curse.

No, the teaching of Jesus most emphatically does not form an exception to the teaching of the Bible regarding the universal sinfulness of mankind. According to the whole of the Bible, and particularly according to Jesus, mankind is lost in sin.

The Bible does not say that just in some far-off, general terms. It brings it right home to every man. It brings it right home to you. According to the Bible, you are lost in sin today – unless you have been saved by God's grace.

How do you know that you are lost in sin? How do we all know that we are sinners?

Well, our own heart condemns us. We know it in that way except when our consciences have become seared as with a hot iron. But there is also Another that tells us we are sinners. Our own heart condemns us, but God is greater than our heart.[1] God has told us we are sinners; He has told us in His own holy Word from beginning to end. Well may the Apostle John say, in view of the whole of the Bible: 'If we say that we have not sinned, we make him a liar.'[2]

God is not a liar, my friends. The whole Bible is right. This world is lost in sin, and you too are lost in sin unless the Holy Spirit has led you or is leading you at this hour to have recourse to God's grace which has been extended you freely and wonderfully in Jesus Christ our Lord.

[1] I John 3:20.   [2] I John 1:10.

18: The Consequences of the Fall of Man

WE OBSERVED IN THE PRECEDING ONE OF THESE little talks that according to the Bible all men are sinners. We observed particularly that the teaching of Jesus forms no exception whatever to this Biblical condemnation of mankind. In His teaching just as in the rest of the Bible we are told that mankind is lost in sin.

Yet according to Jesus that universal sinfulness of mankind is not something that belongs to man just because he is man. It is by no means a necessary part of human nature as such.

There are two ways at least in which we can show from the teaching of Jesus that it is not.

In the first place, Jesus commands His disciples to be perfect as their heavenly Father is perfect.[1] He could not have commanded them to be something which it was never the intention of God that they should be. Therefore sin is not a necessary part of human nature.

In the second place, Jesus Himself presents one example of a man without sin – a person truly having a human nature and yet having no sin. That also shows plainly that sin does not necessarily belong to human nature as such.

The example of a sinless man which Jesus presents is the example of Himself. In the words of Jesus as recorded in the Gospels there is no trace of any consciousness of sin. Jesus taught His disciples to pray, 'Forgive us our debts',[2] but He did not pray that prayer Himself. He says to His disciples, 'If ye then, being evil,'[3] but He did not say, 'If

[1] Matt. 5:48.   [2] Matt. 6:12.   [3] Matt. 7:11.

we, then, being evil'. He did not include Himself in that sinfulness which He attributes to other men. We have here only one instance of a very strange thing that runs all through the words of Jesus as they are recorded in the Gospels – namely, the strange separation which Jesus always preserves between Himself and His hearers in the matter of the relationship to God and in particular in the matter of sin. Jesus never says 'Our Father' to God, joining Himself with His disciples in that word 'our', and certainly He never joins Himself with His disciples in any confession of sin. I think we have sometimes failed to give sufficient attention to that stupendous fact. Imagine any other teacher saying to his hearers, 'If ye then, being evil'! How abominable that would be on the lips of any other than Jesus! Any other religious teacher would say, 'If we all – you and I – then, being evil, know how to give good gifts unto our children.' But Jesus says, 'If *ye* then, being evil'.

Here as always Jesus separates Himself with the utmost clearness from sinful humanity. All mankind, He teaches, is lost in sin, but He Himself is without sin. Surely that is a strange fact.

Is it because Jesus was not a man? No, that explanation will not do at all. The Gospels throughout represent Jesus as being truly a man, and Jesus so represents Himself. Well, then, in Jesus we have a man who was without sin. That shows very clearly that sin is no necessary part of human nature; it is not something constitutive of man's nature as man.

A very serious problem, then, arises. If sin is no necessary part of human nature, how comes it that all mankind, save one, are sinners? How are we to explain this strangely uniform reign of sin?

The same problem is also presented by what we have

said in previous lectures in this little series. We have observed that man, as created, was good. God created man in His own image, in knowledge, righteousness, and holiness. Well, then, if God created man good, how comes it that all men now are bad? How did sin pass into all mankind?

That question is no mere theoretical matter; it is no matter of merely curious interest. On the contrary, it is a matter of the greatest practical importance. From wrong answers to the question how all men came to be sinners have come wrong answers to the question what sin is, and from wrong answers to the question what sin is have come continuance in sin and a turning away from the grace of God. I think that it is a matter of very great moment for our souls that we should get this matter straight once for all in our minds.

Here is the question then. Man was created good. How comes it then that all men upon this earth are now bad? What caused this stupendous change from good to bad?

It does seem as though we ought to have at least a hint of the right answer in what we have said in previous talks in this series. We have seen how sin came into the world. It came in through the sin of Adam. If then the Bible tells us that all men, descended from Adam by ordinary generation, are sinners, surely it is natural for us to say that that universal sinfulness of Adam's descendants was due to Adam's sin. Surely it is natural for us to say that Adam's descendants do not begin life sinless as he began it, but that they begin it tainted in some way or other with the sin that Adam committed. A uniform effect seems to demand that unitary cause.

As to the exact way in which all mankind is involved in Adam's sin, there have been differences of opinion in the

Church. Some have held that mankind forms so much of a unity that what Adam did all men actually did. Mankind, these persons have held, was all concentrated in Adam, so that his act was the act of every single one of us.

It is perfectly clear that that view is contradictory both to common sense and to the Bible. Mankind, both according to common sense and according to the Bible, is a plurality of persons, not one person; and therefore it cannot be said that what Adam did was actually done by every one of his descendants. I have done many wrong things in my life, but I did not eat the forbidden fruit in the garden of Eden. That was not done by me; it was done by another person, Adam.

How comes it, then, that all mankind and not merely Adam is involved in Adam's first sin?

I am going to quote to you what the Shorter Catechism says on that point, and then I am going to ask you whether what the Shorter Catechism says is or is not in accordance with the Bible.

'Did all mankind fall in Adam's first transgression?' So the question reads. Here is the answer. 'The covenant being made with Adam, not only for himself, but for his posterity, all mankind, descending from him by ordinary generation, sinned in him, and fell with him, in his first transgression.'

You will remember what is here meant by the covenant. It is the covenant of works or the covenant of life, which we observed to be so very simple in its terms. If Adam kept perfectly the commandments of God – so the covenant ran – he would have life; if he disobeyed he would have death.

But now the Shorter Cathechism says that that covenant

was made with Adam not only for himself but for his posterity. Has it Biblical warrant for saying so?

I think that even the Book of Genesis, in which the fall of Adam is narrated, indicates rather clearly that the Shorter Catechism has perfectly good Biblical warrant. If Adam transgressed, he was to die. Death was to be the punishment of disobedience. Well, he did transgress. What then happened? Was Adam the only one who died? Did his descendants begin where he began? Did they have placed before them all over again that same alternative between death and life that was placed before Adam? Not at all! The Book of Genesis indicates the contrary very clearly. No, the descendants of Adam already, before they individually made any choices at all, had that penalty of death resting upon them. The Book of Genesis just seems to take that as a matter of course.

What, then, does that mean? It means that when that covenant of life was made with Adam it was made with him as the divinely appointed representative of the race. If he obeyed the commandments of God, the whole race of his descendants would have life; if he disobeyed, the whole race would have death. I do not see how the narrative, when you take it as a whole, can mean anything else.

That view of the matter, presupposed in the Book of Genesis, becomes more explicit in certain important passages of the New Testament. In the latter part of the fifth chapter of Romans, in particular, the Apostle Paul makes it plain. 'Through one trespass,' he there says, 'the judgment came unto all men to condemnation.'[1] 'Through the one man's disobedience,' he says in the next verse, 'the many were made sinners.'[2] In these words and all through

[1] Rom. 5:18. Revised Version.   [2] Rom. 5:19. Revised Version.

this passage we have the great doctrine that when Adam sinned he sinned as the representative of the race, so that it is quite correct to say that all mankind sinned in him and fell with him in his first transgression.

All mankind did not actually sin when Adam sinned, because all mankind did not yet exist. We cannot say that Adam's descendants by any act of their own wills ate the forbidden fruit, because when the forbidden fruit was eaten their own wills and their own personalities were not yet in existence. There is no such thing, strictly speaking, as a collective will of humanity, and therefore it is not correct to say that the collective will of humanity performed that sinful act.

But how comparatively slight is the error of those who say that there is a collective will of humanity and that that collective will of humanity performed that sinful act, compared with the error of those who say that humanity was not involved in Adam's sin at all! How slight is the error of those who say that all mankind *actually* sinned when Adam sinned, compared to the error of those who say that all mankind did not sin at all, did not sin in any sense, when Adam sinned! The Bible plainly teaches that Adam sinned as the representative of all mankind, and that the consequences which his first sin had for him himself it had also for all his posterity.

Adam was the representative of all mankind by appointment of God. We cannot fathom the divine counsels sufficiently to say exactly why God made such an appointment, but we can see that there was something very fitting about it. There is a profound and mysterious connection between the parent and the child. So there is a profound and mysterious connection between Adam and the whole race of his descendants. If he had been made the representative of angels or of some equally divers order of beings, then indeed we should find it difficult to detect anything fitting in such an arrangement; but when he was made the representative of his own descendants, that is surely in analogy with other things that God does, and we can in contemplating it detect something of the perfect wisdom and harmony to be found in all God's dealings with His creatures.

When Adam sinned, then, all mankind sinned in him and fell with him. All the consequences which his first transgression had for him it had also for his posterity.

It is quite right, therefore, when the next question in the Shorter Catechism reads not 'Into what estate did the fall bring Adam?' but 'Into what estate did the fall bring mankind?' We must study now the consequences of Adam's first sin for all humanity.

The Shorter Catechism says in its answer to the question just quoted that those consequences of Adam's first sin may be summed up if we say that the fall brought mankind into an estate of sin and misery.

Wherein, then, consists the sinfulness of that estate whereinto the fall brought mankind?

The answer of the Shorter Catechism to that question is one of the weightiest in the whole of that wonderful summary of Bible teaching. I trust you will attend to it very carefully with me now; and then if you have questions in your mind about it and difficulties regarding it I trust you will let me try in the following talk to show you how, despite those questions and despite those difficulties, the teaching of the Bible on this great subject stands triumphantly and majestically against the assaults of opposing views. Particularly do I want you to see that these matters are not just theological subtleties, but are of profound moment for every man and every woman and every child.

Let us then take as the basis of our discussion that weighty answer in the Shorter Catechism to the question regarding the sinfulness of the estate into which the fall brought mankind. 'The sinfulness of that estate whereinto man fell,' says the Shorter Catechism, 'consists in, the guilt of Adam's first sin, the want of original righteousness, and the corruption of his whole nature, which is commonly called original sin; together with all actual transgressions which proceed from it.'

The first thing that this answer says is that the *guilt* of Adam's first sin rested upon all his descendants. Every man descended from Adam by ordinary generation comes into the world bearing the awful penalty which God pronounced upon disobedience.

At this point some of you may hold up your hands in horror. How, you may say, can one person bear the guilt of another person's sin? How can we possibly suppose that before infants have done anything either good or bad they yet are punished because of what Adam did so long ago?

Well, I should just like to point out to you that if it is impossible in the nature of things for one person to bear the guilt of another person's sins, then we have none of us the slightest hope of being saved and the gospel is all a delusion and a snare. At the heart of the gospel is the teaching of the Bible to the effect that Jesus Christ, quite without sin Himself, bore the guilt of our sins upon the Cross. If that be true, then we cannot pronounce it impossible that one person should bear the guilt of another person's sins.

The Apostle Paul insists upon this analogy in the latter part of the fifth chapter of Romans. In that part of that chapter we find set forth the great Scripture doctrine that is called the doctrine of imputation.

That doctrine, if you take it as the Bible sets it forth as a whole, involves three great acts of imputation. First, Adam's first sin is imputed to his descendants. Second, the sins of saved people are imputed to Christ. Third, Christ's righteousness is imputed to saved people.

When the Bible teaches that the sins of saved people are imputed to Christ, that means that Christ on the Cross bore the penalty rightly resting on saved people. He was not deserving of death; He had not sinned at all. Yet He suffered as though He had sinned. God treated Him as though He had sinned, although He was not a sinner. The sin for which He died was not a sin that He had committed; it was our sin that was imputed to Him.

So, when the Bible teaches that Christ's righteousness is imputed to saved people, that does not mean that the saved people are then actually righteous. On the contrary, they are sinners. But they receive the blessed reward of life which Christ's righteousness deserved. Christ's righteousness is not actually theirs, but it is imputed to them.

So, finally, when the Bible teaches that Adam's first transgression was imputed to his descendants, that does not mean that those descendants had actually committed that first transgression. But the penalty which God pronounced upon that sin of Adam rested upon them. Adam committed that first transgression as their representative. They as well as he bore the penalty.

Listen to the wonderfully clear way in which that is taught in the fifth chapter of Romans:

'So then as through one trespass the judgment came unto all men to condemnation; even so through one act of
[216]

righteousness the free gift came unto all men to justifica-
tion of life. For as through the one man's disobedience the
many were made sinners, even so through the obedience of
the one shall the many be made righteous.'[1]

'Through one trespass the judgment came unto all men
to condemnation . . . through the one man's disobedience
the many were made sinners' – there we have, expressed
with a clearness that could scarcely be surpassed, the doctrine of the imputation of Adam's sin to his posterity. All
mankind, descended from Adam by ordinary generation,
bore the penalty which God pronounced upon Adam's first
transgression.

Does, then, that doctrine of the imputation of Adam's
sin to his posterity mean that the descendants of Adam,
though themselves good, yet suffer the penalty of Adam's
sin? Does it mean that good people, because of what Adam
did so long ago, are treated by God as though they were
bad, suffering, although they are good, many miseries in
this life and the pains of hell forever?

No, indeed, it does not mean that at all. On the contrary,
every person who suffers the penalty of Adam's sin is also
himself bad. Indeed, badness is necessarily involved in
that penalty itself.

God said to Adam that if he disobeyed he would die.
What is the meaning of that death? Well, it includes
physical death; there is no question about that. But, alas,
it also includes far more than physical death. It includes
spiritual death; it includes the death of the soul unto
things that are good; it includes the death of the soul
unto God. The dreadful penalty of that sin of Adam was

[1] Rom. 5:18 f.

that Adam and his descendants became dead in trespasses and sins.

When I say that, I do not mean that God is the author of sin, either the sin that comes because of prior sin or any other kind of sin. But I do mean that as a just penalty of Adam's sin, God withdrew His favour, and the souls of all mankind became spiritually dead.

That spiritual deadness is described in the Shorter Catechism in the words that follow the words, 'the guilt of Adam's first sin', which we have been trying to expound. 'The sinfulness of that estate whereinto man fell,' says the Shorter Catechism, 'consists in, the guilt of Adam's first sin, the want of original righteousness, and the corruption of his whole nature, which is commonly called original sin; together with all actual transgressions which proceed from it.' The want of original righteousness and the corruption of man's whole nature, into which the fall brought mankind, constitute spiritual death.

That want of original righteousness, that corruption of man's whole nature, that spiritual death, is itself sin. It is not just the basis for sin, the substratum of sin, the root out of which sin comes. It is, indeed, all that. All actual transgressions proceed from it. But it is more than the basis or the substratum of sin. It is itself sin. The soul that is spiritually dead, the soul that is corrupt with that dreadful corruption, is no longer sinful merely with the imputed guilt of Adam's first transgression. No it is sinful with its own sinfulness. It is guilty not only because of Adam's guilt but also because of its own sin. It deserves eternal punishment because it itself is now sinful.

Many questions arise in many persons' minds regarding that Scripture doctrine of original sin. 'Is a man really responsible,' they ask, 'for a corruption of his nature that he cannot help, a corruption of his nature with which he was born? Can he really be commanded to do something that he has no ability to do? Can he really be commanded to be something that he cannot be?'

If such questions arise in your mind, I ask you to attend to what will be said in the following talk.

19: What is Original Sin?

IN THE LAST TALK WE SPOKE OF THE WAY IN WHICH all men came to be sinners. God made a covenant with Adam. If he obeyed perfectly the commandments of God, he was to have life. If he disobeyed, he was to die. The death with which he was to die was not only physical death. It was also spiritual death. It meant the death of the soul to things that were good and to God, a profound corruption of man's whole nature.

That covenant, we observed further was made with Adam not only for himself but for his posterity. It was made with Adam as the representative of the whole human race, and whatever it meant for Adam, therefore, it meant for all mankind. If he had kept the covenant, not only he but all mankind would have had eternal life. There would have been no more probation; there would have been no more jeopardy. Mankind would not only have had righteousness as it had had when Adam was created, but it would now have had an assured righteousness; the very possibility of sinning would have been removed.

As a matter of fact, however, Adam did not keep the covenant; he sinned against God by eating the forbidden fruit. The result was that not only he but all mankind received the dreadful penalty pronounced against disobedience. The penalty was death – not only physical death but also the far more terrible spiritual death, the death of the soul to things that are good, the death of the soul to God.

Thus all mankind through the fall has become corrupt

and utterly unable to please God. The individual sins that men commit are but manifestations of that profound corruption of man's nature. The fruit is corrupt because the tree is corrupt.

Such, according to the Shorter Catechism, and according to the Bible, is the sinfulness of that estate whereinto man fell.

But the Shorter Catechism, again in accordance with the Bible, says that the estate whereinto man fell was an estate not only of sin but also of misery.

What, then, is the misery of that estate whereinto man fell? The Shorter Catechism gives the answer with words which at least are perfectly easy to understand. 'All mankind,' it says, 'by their fall, lost communion with God, are under his wrath and curse, and so made liable to all the miseries of this life, to death itself, and to the pains of hell for ever.'

Do you think we need elaborate discussion to prove that that answer is in accordance with the Bible? I am inclined to think not, my friends. Just run over the Bible in your mind, and you will see that the Shorter Catechism is perfectly right.

'All mankind by their fall lost communion with God.' What a vivid picture of that loss we have in the Book of Genesis:

'And they [Adam and Eve] heard the voice of the Lord God walking in the garden in the cool of the day: and Adam and his wife hid themselves from the presence of the Lord God amongst the trees in the garden.'[1]

Gone were the days when God conversed with Adam freely as with His child; gone was the joy which Adam

[1] Gen. 3:8.

formerly had in the presence of God. He hid himself now from God, and soon a flaming sword separated him from the garden where he had had communion with his heavenly Father. The Bible certainly loses no time in making it clear that all mankind by their fall lost communion with God.

The Bible makes it equally clear that all mankind by their fall came under God's wrath and curse. The doctrine of the wrath of God is not a popular doctrine, but there is no doctrine that is more utterly pervasive in the Bible. Paul devotes to it a large part of three chapters out of the eight chapters in his great Epistle to the Romans which he devotes to the exposition of his message of salvation, and he is at particular pains to show that the wrath of God rests upon all men except those who have been saved by God's grace. But there is nothing peculiar within the Bible in that great passage in the first three chapters of Romans. That passage only puts in a comprehensive way what is presupposed from Genesis to Revelation and becomes explicit in passages almost beyond number.

Does the teaching of Jesus form any exception to the otherwise pervasive presentation of the wrath of God in the Bible? Well, you might think so if you listened only to what modern sentimentality says about Jesus of Nazareth. The men of the world, who have never been born again, who have never come under the conviction of sin, have reconstructed a Jesus to suit themselves, a feeble sentimentalist who preached only the love of God and had nothing to say about God's wrath. But very different was the real Jesus, the Jesus who is presented to us in our sources of historical information. The real Jesus certainly proclaimed a God who, as the Old Testament which He revered as God's Word says, is a 'consuming fire'.[1] Very

[1] Deut. 4:24. Compare Heb. 12:29.

terrible was Jesus' own anger as the Gospels describe it, a profound burning indignation against sin; and very terrible is the anger of the God whom He proclaimed as the Ruler of heaven and earth. No, you certainly cannot escape from the teaching of the Bible about the wrath of God by appealing to Jesus of Nazareth. The most terrible even among the Biblical presentations of God's wrath are those that are found in our blessed Saviour's words.

Finally the Shorter Catechism says that all mankind by their fall are 'made liable to all the miseries of this life, to death itself, and to the pains of hell for ever'. Here again the Biblical warrant is perfectly plain, and here again at the heart of the Biblical warrant is to be found what was said by Jesus. Where do you find the most terrible descriptions of hell in the whole of the Bible? In the Book of Revelation, perhaps you may say. Well, I am not sure. At least equally terrible are those that are found in the teaching of Jesus. It is Jesus who speaks of the sin that shall not be forgiven either in this world or that which is to come; it is Jesus who speaks of the worm that dieth not and the fire that is not quenched;[1] it is Jesus who has given us the story of the rich man and Lazarus[2] and of the great gulf between them; it is Jesus who says that it is profitable for a man to enter into life having one eye rather than having two eyes to be cast into hell fire.[3] Just let your mind run through the teaching of Jesus, and I think you will really be surprised to find how pervasive in His teaching is the thought of hell. It appears in the Sermon on the Mount; it appears of course in the great judgment chapter, the twenty-fifth of Matthew; it appears in passages too numerous to mention. It is not somewhere on the circum-

[1] Mk. 9:48.   [2] Lk. 16:19–31.   [3] Matt. 18:9.

ference of His teaching, but is at the very heart and core of it.

I do not believe we always understand quite clearly enough how great is the divergence at this point between the teaching of Jesus and current preaching both at home and on the mission field. Men are interested today in this world. They have lost the consciousness of sin, and having lost the consciousness of sin they have lost the fear of hell. They have tried to make of Christianity a religion of this world. They have excogitated the so-called 'social gospel'. They have come to regard Christianity just as a programme for setting up the conditions of the kingdom of God upon this earth, and they are tremendously impatient when any-one looks upon it as a means of entering into heaven and escaping hell.

The strange thing about this way of thinking is not that men engage in it. The thought of hell is of course not palat-able to men who have never been born again; it is an offence to the natural man. But what is indeed strange is that in support of this this-worldly way of thinking, men should appeal to Jesus of Nazareth.

As a matter of fact the teaching of Jesus centres alto-gether in the thought of heaven and of hell:

'Lay not up for yourselves treasures upon earth, where moth and rust doth corrupt, and where thieves break through and steal: but lay up for yourselves treasures in heaven, where neither moth nor rust doth corrupt, and where thieves do not break through nor steal: for where your treasure is, there will be your heart also.'[1]

'Be not afraid of them that kill the body, and after that have no more that they can do. But I will forewarn you

[1] Matt. 6:19-21.

whom ye shall fear: Fear him, which after he hath killed hath power to cast into hell; yea, I say unto you, fear him.'[1] These words are typical of all of Jesus' teaching. The teaching of Jesus is intensely other-worldly. A man who regards it as consisting essentially in a programme for this world has not got the slightest inkling of its meaning. Let not anyone who thinks that fear of hell should be put out of the mind of unregenerate men ever suppose that he has the slightest understanding of what Jesus came into the world to say and do.

But please understand exactly why it is that I am alluding to this subject now. I am not doing so because it is my intention to set forth now what the Bible says about the future life. That would belong to another series of talks. My purpose now is somewhat different. I have mentioned the Biblical teaching about hell simply because it is necessary in order that you may understand the Biblical teaching about sin. The awfulness of the punishment of sin shows as nothing else could well do how heinous a thing sin really is in the sight of God.

I have tried to present to you in bare outline something like the whole picture – man guilty with the imputed guilt of Adam's first sin, man suffering therefore the death that is the penalty of that sin, not only physical death but also that spiritual death that consists in the corruption of man's whole nature and in his total inability to please God, man bringing forth out of his corrupt heart individual acts of transgression without number, man facing eternal punishment in hell. That is the picture that runs all through the Bible. Mankind, according to the Bible, is a lost race, lost in sin; and sin is not just a misfortune, but is something that

[1] Lk. 12:4 f.

calls forth the white heat of the divine indignation. Before the awful justice of God no unclean thing can stand; and man is unclean, transgressor against God's holy law, subject justly to its awful penalty.

As I try to present that picture to you, I think you as well as I are impressed with the fact that the men of the present day for the most part will have none of it. They will not admit at all that mankind is lost in sin. I remember a service that I attended some years ago in a little church in a pretty village. The preacher was distinctly above the average in culture and in moral fervour. I do not remember his sermon (except that it was a glorification of man); but I do remember something that he said in his prayer. He quoted that verse from Jeremiah to the effect that the heart of man is 'deceitful above all things, and desperately wicked',[1] and then he said in his prayer, as nearly as I can remember his words: 'O Lord, thou knowest that we no longer accept this interpretation, but now think that man does what is right if only he knows the way.' Well, that was at least being frank about the matter. We have a good opinion of ourselves these days, and if so, why should we not let the Lord in on our secret? Why should we go on quoting with a sanctimonious air confessions of sin from the Bible if we really do not believe a word of them? I think the prayer of that village preacher was bad – very bad – but I also think that perhaps it was not *so* bad perhaps as the prayers of those preachers who have really rejected the central message of the Bible just as completely as he had and yet conceal the fact by the use of traditional language. At least that prayer raised the issue clearly between the Biblical view of sin and the paganism of the modern creed, 'I believe in man'.

[1] Jer. 17:9.

At the very foundation of all that the Bible says is this sad truth – that mankind is lost in sin.

I want to say just a little more to you about that truth before I go on to speak of salvation from sin.

The Bible teaches, we have observed, that every man comes into the world a sinner, with a corruption of nature out of which all individual transgressions proceed. That is the doctrine of original sin. It is against that doctrine of original sin that the chief attack has been made; and I want to say a few words to you about the attack in order that the Bible doctrine which is attacked may become the more clear.

The attack against the doctrine of original sin has come to be connected with the name of a British monk who lived in the latter part of the fourth and the early part of the fifth century after Christ. His name was Pelagius. From him the whole family of the Pelagians is named. It is a numerous family. There are millions of Pelagians living today, and most of them never knew that such a person as Pelagius ever lived.

Like many other people who have wrought untold harm to the souls of men, Pelagius seems to have been himself a very respectable gentleman. His great opponent was careful to say, I believe, that he recognized the attractiveness of Pelagius' life in many respects and certainly had no personal grudge against him.

The opponent of Pelagius was one of the greatest men in the whole history of the Christian Church. His name was Augustine. The controversy between Augustine and Pelagius is one of the most famous controversies ever known in human history. Its fame is quite just. In that Pelagian controversy an issue was fought out that is at the very vitals of the Christian Church.

Fortunately the story of the controversy has been told for us by one of the greatest masters in the field of the history of doctrine, the late Professor Benjamin Breckinridge Warfield, in an essay entitled 'Augustine and the Pelagian Controversy' which he contributed originally to the *Library of the Nicene and Post-Nicene Fathers* and which is now reprinted in the volume entitled *Studies in Tertullian and Augustine* in his collected works. To Dr Warfield I am indebted, to a very considerable extent, for what I am now saying regarding Pelagius. That brings me to confess in general with regard to this little series of talks that I am laying no claim to originality, and that before every talk I obtain great profit, for example, from reading over the relevant section in the great work on Systematic Theology by Charles Hodge. It would be a fine thing if some of you would read over that great work with me. I think it is a very great mistake indeed for us to suppose that nobody before our day ever understood anything of what the Bible teaches; and I for my part rejoice greatly in trying to stand in the great current of the Reformed Faith. If I can show you a little bit of what that great system of doctrine is and a little bit of the basis for it in the Word of God, the purpose of these talks will have been fully attained.

But it is time for us to return to Pelagius and his attack on the Biblical doctrine of original sin.

In contravention of that doctrine – though of course he supposed, however erroneously, that his teaching was in accordance with the Bible – Pelagius said that every man, far from being born with a corrupt nature, begins life practically where Adam began it, being perfectly able to choose either good or evil. Indeed, said he, if a man has not that ability to choose either good or evil, he cannot be held responsible for his acts. He is not responsible for anything that he cannot help. Thus if people were – as, said Pelagius, they are not – born with a corrupt nature, that corruption of nature would not be sin. Sin is just a matter of individual acts; it appears only in those cases where a man has ability to choose either good or evil and where as a matter of fact he chooses evil instead of good.

It seems evident that that doctrine of Pelagius involves at least two things. In the first place, it involves a certain view of what sin is; and in the second place, it involves a denial of any appreciable effects of Adam's sin upon his posterity.

Let us look at these two things for a minute or two in turn.

In the first place, let us look at this Pelagian notion that sin inheres only in sinful acts and that a man cannot be blamed for a corruption of nature that he cannot help.

When we do look at it, we observe that it is really quite absurd. Suppose a man has committed a murder or a robbery. Suppose we are old-fashioned enough to tell him that we think he ought not to have done it. What does he say to us if, in accordance with Pelagius' teaching, he supposes that a man cannot be blamed for that corruption of nature that underlies his individual acts?

Why, he says to us that we are quite wrong in blaming him. 'Do you blame me,' he says, 'for committing that murder or that robbery? You ought not to blame me. I admit that murder and robbery do seem to be bad actions; but then, you see, I am a bad man and so I could not help committing those bad actions. Well, if I could not help it I am not to be blamed for it. I simply acted in accordance with my nature. If a good man commits bad actions you can blame him, but if a bad man does so that is only to be expected; he is only acting in accordance with his nature, and no blame ought to be attached to him for doing what he does.'

Well, perhaps I am impressed with what my murderer friend says to me; but still I cannot get rid of the feeling that murder and robbery are reprehensible, and that folks ought not to indulge in them to any great extent. So I say to myself that surely I ought to be able to blame *somebody* for committing murders or for committing robberies. Now my murderer friend has told me that I can blame good people if they commit murders or robberies. So I go out hopefully on the search for such people. But then I make a truly startling discovery – the discovery that good people do not commit murders or robberies. So there is nobody at all whom I can blame for those acts. I cannot blame bad people for them, because they cannot help committing them; they commit them merely in accordance with their nature: and I cannot blame good people for committing them, because good people do not commit them at all. So apparently I was wrong in thinking that any moral blame attached to such acts. Murder and robbery are apparently not deserving of blame after all.

Perhaps you say that that conclusion is absurd. Well, it may be absurd; but it is exactly the conclusion that is dominant to an alarming extent in the thought of the present day. Hosts of people deny the whole notion of moral obligation; they deny that anybody can really be blamed for murder or robbery or adultery or any other sin. Why do they do so? They do so for the simple reason that they cannot accept either the Pelagian notion or the Biblical notion of sin; and so they just deny that there is any such thing as sin.

They cannot, in the first place, accept the Pelagian notion that bad actions are due simply to a bad choice of a will that had perfect ability to choose either bad or good. The facts are dead against that Pelagian notion. Even an elementary study of criminology shows that back of the bad action lies a bad nature of the criminal and, for that matter – though there we are anticipating another point – a bad nature with which the criminal was born.

But then these people about whom I am speaking also reject the Biblical doctrine. They reject the doctrine that bad actions springing from a bad nature, and indeed the bad nature itself, are worthy of blame.

Well, then, if bad actions that spring from a bad nature of the criminal are not subject to moral reprobation, and if the bad nature itself is also not a thing for which the criminal can be blamed, and if people with a good nature do not commit bad actions, it follows that nothing at all and no one at all can be blamed, and we have simply the profoundly anti-moral doctrine of modern criminology that there is no such thing as moral obligation and that crime is a disease.

The only escape from the abyss of that doctrine, which means if it is permanently dominant the ruin of civilization, to say nothing of what may come in another world, is simply to fall back upon the Biblical doctrine that a man most emphatically can be blamed for things that he cannot help and in particular that he most emphatically can be blamed, and is blamed by God, for a sinful nature with which he was born.

The Bible plainly teaches in the first place that sinful actions come from a corrupt nature of the man who commits them, and in the second place that that corruption of nature is itself sin. But I am going to ask you to look at this matter a little more fully at the beginning of the next talk, in order that then, having spoken of sin, we may go on to speak of salvation.

20: Sinners Saved by Grace

AT THE CLOSE OF THE LAST TALK, WE WERE SPEAK-
ing of a great attack which has been made upon the Biblical doctrine of original sin.

The attack was first made in the early fifth century by
Pelagius, the opponent of Augustine, but it has been made
in one form or another in every age of the Christian
Church, and it is being made with particular insistence
today.

Pelagianism, we observed, involves a certain view, first,
as to what sin is, and, second, as to the effects of Adam's
sin upon his posterity. I was speaking to you at the close
of the last talk about the former of these two subjects –
namely, the Pelagian view of the nature of sin.

According to the Pelagian view, certainly according to
the logic of that way of thinking, sin is just a matter of individual acts; it is not a matter of the underlying state of
the soul. The will, according to Pelagianism, has the power
of self-determination at any moment, and it is the bad use
of that power of self-determination that is to be called sin.

Upon that power of self-determination, Pelagians say,
moral responsibility depends. A man, they say, cannot be
held responsible for what he cannot help. Therefore if his
individual acts did come inevitably from the underlying
state of his nature, he would not be responsible either for
those individual acts or for the underlying state of his
nature from which they came. As a matter of fact, Pelagians hold, no such state of affairs exists, man being as a

matter of fact perfectly able at any time to choose either good or evil.

According to the Augustinian view of sin, on the other hand, individual wrong choices do most emphatically come from the underlying state of the person who engages in them. The will most emphatically is not free in the sense that it can choose this or that, no matter what the nature of the person doing the choosing may be.

So far the Augustinian view of sin is in accordance, I suppose, with what is said by most of the psychologists and criminologists of the present day.

But it differs from what is said by those psychologists and criminologists in holding that a man most emphatically is morally responsible for wrong choices springing out of his evil nature, and that he is most emphatically responsible for the evil nature out of which those wrong choices spring. Augustinianism differs, in other words, both from Pelagianism and from modern psychology in holding that a man is responsible for things that he cannot help. If he is a bad man, if he has a bad nature, he is responsible for that bad nature, no matter how it came to be bad. Sin, according to Augustinianism, is not just a matter of individual actions; it also inheres in the state underlying the actions. A man who commits a bad action cannot, according to Augustinianism, be excused on the ground that he is and always has been a bad man; on the contrary, a bad man, even aside from any particular bad actions, is justly subject to reprobation and abhorrence by man and by God. Both the bad actions and also the bad state from which the bad actions come are, according to Augustine, sin.

Is that Augustinian view the view of the Bible? I think that question needs only to be raised in order to be answered. I am just going to quote one passage and then I am going to ask you whether that passage does not sum up the teaching of the whole Bible on this point. The passage which I am going to quote is not taken from what are sometimes supposed to be the more philosophical or theological parts of the Bible. It is taken from the teaching of Jesus as recorded in the Synoptic Gospels. Yet it refutes the whole Pelagian view of the freedom of the will, the whole Pelagian notion that sin is a matter only of individual actions; and it refutes that whole notion more effectively than could be done by entire volumes of philosophy. Here is the passage to which I refer:

'Either make the tree good, and his fruit good; or else make the tree corrupt, and his fruit corrupt: for the tree is known by his fruit. O generation of vipers, how can ye, being evil, speak good things? for out of the abundance of the heart the mouth speaketh. A good man out of the good treasure of the heart bringeth forth good things: and an evil man out of the evil treasure bringeth forth evil things.'[1]

In the light of these words of Jesus, so simple and so profound, how utterly shallow the whole Pelagian view of the will and of sin is seen to be! According to Jesus, evil actions come from an evil heart, and both the actions and the heart from which they come are sinful.

That view is the view of the whole Bible. There is in the Bible from beginning to end no shadow of comfort for the shallow notion that sin is a matter only of individual choices and that a bad man can, without being changed within, suddenly bring forth good actions. No, the Bible everywhere finds the root of evil in the heart, and by the

[1] Matt. 12:33-35.

heart it does not mean just the feelings but the whole inner life of man. The heart of man, it tells us, is deceitful above all things and desperately wicked, and because of that, man is a sinner in the sight of God.

The question may perhaps arise at this point in the minds of some of you whether such a view does not do away with personal freedom and personal responsibility.

Well, what do we mean by personal freedom? Do we mean by it a freedom of the will as an unaccountable something or other that swings around loosely inside of a man without any reference to the rest of the man and in particular without any reference to the question whether the nature of the man is good or bad? If we mean that, we mean something that not only is quite absurd but also destroys that personal freedom that it started out to defend. The thing that makes an action a personal action is just that it proceeds from the whole nature of the man that engages in it. If the will were really free in the sense that it were without roots in the underlying being of the man who wills, then its choices would not be personal choices at all but would be just the meaningless swinging hither and yon of a pendulum governed by blind chance. As a matter of fact, there is no such thing as the will, considered as a separate something-or-other inside of a man; but what we call the will is just the whole man willing, as what we call the intellect is the whole man thinking and what we call the feelings is the whole man feeling. What we really ought to mean, therefore, when we speak of the freedom of the will, is rather the freedom of the man. A man is free and therefore morally responsible when his actions spring from his own nature and when he is aware of the fact that they are his own actions. If, indeed, a man is compelled, by actual direct physical impulsion, to do something against his will, then that is not really his own personal act and he is not morally responsible for it; but if his will itself is determined by his own nature, then no matter how inevitable the thing that he does may be it is most emphatically his own personal act and he most emphatically is morally responsible for it. An evil man inevitably performs evil actions; the thing is as certain as that a corrupt tree will bring forth corrupt fruit: but the evil man performs those evil actions because he wants to perform them; they are his own free personal acts and he is responsible for them in the sight of God.

Such is not only sound philosophy and sound common sense, but it is plainly the teaching of the Bible from Genesis to Revelation.

Still, however, an objection may perhaps remain. Can a man really be blamed for something that he cannot help? Can he be blamed for an evil nature which he never was without and with which, indeed, he was born?

With regard to that objection I should just like to point out this – that if a person cannot be blamed for an evil nature, then it follows with an inevitable logic that he cannot be praised for a good nature.

Do you say that a person cannot be blamed for a nature that he always had, a nature that underlies all his individual acts? Well, then, if that principle is true of blame it is also true of praise. Can a person be praised for a nature that he always had, a nature that he did not produce? Do you say, No? Well, then, how about God? His good actions spring inevitably from His infinitely good nature. Is He then not to be praised? Ask the heavenly hosts who delight ever to sing His praises before the throne; ask all the saints who bless Him for His excellent name. How reads the last of the Psalms:

'Praise ye the Lord. Praise God in his sanctuary: praise him in the firmament of his power.

Praise him for his mighty acts: praise him according to his excellent greatness.

Praise him with the sound of the trumpet: praise him with the psaltery and harp.

Praise him with the timbrel and dance: praise him with stringed instruments and organs.

Praise him upon the loud cymbals: praise him upon the high-sounding cymbals.

Let everything that hath breath praise the Lord. Praise ye the Lord.'

On the Pelagian theory that chorus of praise would have to be silenced. God did not make Himself good; He always was good; His good actions come, with a certainty than which nothing can be more certain, from His good nature: therefore, on the Pelagian theory, let Him not be praised!

But perhaps you say that God's nature is so different from ours that we cannot reason from what is true about Him to what is true about us. Well, then, how about the good angels? Their good actions spring inevitably from the goodness of their nature, and they did not create their nature, but it was created for them by God. Are they then not to be praised? How about the saints also who have gone to their reward? Surely for them the possibility of sinning is over; they are as perfectly good as the good angels are; in their case, as in the case of the good angels, good actions spring from an underlying goodness of nature. And in their case also, unless the Bible is altogether wrong, the goodness of their nature is not a product of their own endeavours but a gift of God. It was given to them in the

[238]

new birth. Yet surely they are to be pronounced blessed and gloriously free.

Do you not see, my friends, how absurd is this Pelagian notion that moral praise or blame is not to be applied to the underlying nature of persons but only to their individual acts? The true state of the case is that the individual acts obtain their moral quality largely because of their connection with the underlying nature of the person who engages in them. A person is good if his nature is good, no matter how it came to be good, and a person is bad if his nature is bad, no matter how it came to be bad. So bad men are sinners in the sight of God, and subject to His just wrath and curse, even though they were born bad.

That brings us to the second part of the Pelagian contention. If Pelagianism holds a shallow view regarding the question what sin is, it also holds a shallow view regarding the sin of the human race. It denies that Adam's sin had any very appreciable effects for his posterity. Every man, it holds, begins life practically where Adam began it, with complete ability to choose either good or evil. Thus it rejects the whole doctrine of original sin; it rejects the whole doctrine that all men descended from Adam by ordinary generation come into the world with a corrupt nature which then leads inevitably to individual acts of sin.

Of course, an obvious objection faces any such Pelagian view. If all men descended from Adam by ordinary generation come into the world without a corrupt nature and with a full ability to choose good instead of evil, why is it that all men without exception choose evil; why is it that all men are sinners? If the question whether men shall be righteous or sinners depends upon the choice of the individual men, and if every man has full ability to choose one way or the other, it does seem exceedingly strange that all men have happened to choose the same way. The chances according to any mathematical law of averages would be far more than ten billion times ten billion to one against any such result.

To this objection I am not sure whether Pelagius did or did not reply that as a matter of fact some men have chosen the right. I am not quite sure whether he did or did not deny the universal sinfulness of mankind. If he did deny it, he certainly placed himself squarely against the whole of the Bible, as we have already seen. But at any rate Pelagianism can only explain the general reign of sin by the bad example which Adam set. Adam, according to Pelagianism, set a bad example to the race; Christ set a good example. Men are perfectly able to follow either Adam's example or Christ's example. That is just a matter for the choice of the individual human will.

Such are the limits to which both sin and salvation are reduced according to the Pelagian scheme.

Do I need to say that that scheme is radically contrary to the Bible? The Bible from beginning to end plainly teaches that individual sins come from a sinful nature, and that the nature of all men is sinful from their birth. 'Behold, I was shapen in iniquity; and in sin did my mother conceive me' – these words of the Fifty-first Psalm summarize, in the cry of a penitent sinner, a doctrine of sin which runs through the Bible from Genesis to Revelation. Upon that Biblical view of sin depends also the Biblical view of salvation. Does the Bible teach that all Christ did for us is to set us a good example which we are perfectly able to follow without a change of our hearts? The man who thinks so is a man who has not come even to the threshold of the great central truth which the Scriptures contain. 'Ye must be born again,' said Jesus Christ.[1] The man who believes that Jesus spake the truth when He said that must make a clean break with Pelagianism in all its many forms. No, my friends, despite Pelagius and his millions of modern followers, there is no hope whatever for us until we are born again by an act that is not our own; there is no hope that we shall really choose the right until we are made alive from the dead by the blessed act of the Spirit of the living God. To the man who does not see that, the Bible is still a sealed book. At the very foundation of the teaching of the Bible is the great Biblical doctrine of original sin.

That doctrine means that all mankind, since the fall, are totally corrupt and totally unable to please God. I think we ought to pause just there for a minute or two.

The doctrine that is called the doctrine of 'total depravity' is one of the so-called five points of Calvinism. But it is not only one of the five points of Calvinism. It is also one of the things upon which the Bible lays greatest stress. I think it is very important for us to observe exactly what it means.

It does not mean that all men not Christians are at every moment just as bad as they possibly can be. On the contrary it is perfectly consonant with what is also plainly taught in Scripture – that the Spirit of God, by His common grace, restrains even unregenerate men from the full manifestation of the power of evil that dominates them. What then does the doctrine of total depravity mean?

It means, in the first place, that the corruption of fallen man affects all parts of man's nature. His faculties remain, it is true; he is still a man, and as being still a man he is responsible. But all his faculties, all parts of his nature, are

[1] John 3:7.

vitiated by the corruption into which he has fallen. Sin does not reside merely in the body; it does not reside merely in the feelings, or merely in the intellect, or merely in what is sometimes falsely set off from the rest of human nature under the name of the will. But it resides in all of these. The whole life of man, and not merely any one part of it, is corrupt.

In the second place, the Biblical doctrine of total depravity means that nothing that fallen and unregenerate men can do is really well-pleasing to God. Many things that they do are able to please us, with our imperfect standards, but nothing that they do is able to please God; nothing that they do can stand in the white light of His judgment-throne. Some of their actions may be relatively good, but none of them are really good. All of them are affected by the deep depravity of the fallen human nature from which they come.

That may seem to us to be a hard doctrine, but it is plainly taught in the Word of God. Moreover, it receives heartfelt recognition from the truest saints. Ask the men of really holy life in the history of the Christian Church, and they will tell you as they look back upon their lives in the period before they became Christians – even in cases where those lives have seemed to other people to be fine self-sacrificing lives – that all that supposed goodness was just filthy rags in the sight of God. No, my friends, mankind, until regenerated by the mysterious act of the Spirit of God, is unable even for an instant so to live as really to please God.

That brings us to another aspect of the great Biblical doctrine of total depravity. It is found in the complete inability of fallen man to lift himself out of his fallen condition. Fallen man, according to the Bible, is unable to contribute the smallest part to the great change by which he is made to be alive from the dead. Every man in whom that great change takes place does indeed have faith in the Lord Jesus Christ; it is through that personal act of faith that he is united to the Lord Jesus. But the point is that that faith is worked in him by the Holy Spirit of God. Men who are dead in trespasses and sins are utterly unable to have saving faith, just as completely unable as a dead man lying in the tomb is unable to contribute the slightest bit to his resurrection. When a man is born again, the Holy Spirit works faith in him, and he contributes nothing whatever to that blessed result. After he has been born again, he does coöperate with the Spirit of God in the daily battle against sin; after he has been made alive by God, he proceeds to show that he is alive by bringing forth good works: but until he is made alive he can do nothing that is really good; and the act of the Spirit of God by which he is made alive is a resistless and sovereign act.

That is so fundamental in the Bible, the Bible lays such tremendous stress upon it, that it does seem strange that people who believe in the Bible should deny it. As a matter of fact, however, semi-Pelagianism, assigning some part to man in the attainment of salvation, has appeared in a great many different forms in the history of the Church.

You will remember what pure Pelagianism is. According to the out-and-out Pelagian view, man needs no change of nature in order to lay hold upon the gospel and be saved; indeed, the gospel is really not strictly necessary for salvation at all; it merely brings to bear an additional persuasion upon a man in order to induce him to do what is right, and he is perfectly able to do what is right in accordance with the freedom of his own will.

The semi-Pelagian view is a sort of compromise between

that out-and-out Pelagian view and the Augustinian view which is so plainly taught in the Bible. According to the semi-Pelagian view, man's nature is weakened by the fall; and although the weakening which every man derives from Adam is not in itself sin it leads inevitably to sin unless the grace of God intervenes.

Then in addition to this semi-Pelagianism there has been a vast deal of forty-five per cent Pelagianism, forty per cent Pelagianism and Pelagianism in almost every conceivable proportion. Some have held that although fallen man can do nothing positively to save himself, he can choose whether he will resist or accept the proffered grace of God. Thus man does have to do his part, even though it be only a negative part, in the work of salvation.

To all such compromises the Bible opposes its perfectly clear doctrine of the total inability of fallen man and the all-sufficiency of divine grace. Man, according to the Bible, is not merely sick in trespasses and sins; he is not merely in a weakened condition so that he needs divine help: but he is dead in trespasses and sins. He can do absolutely nothing to save himself, and God saves him by the gracious, sovereign act of the new birth. The Bible is a tremendously uncompromising book in this matter of the sin of man and the grace of God.

The Biblical doctrine of the grace of God does not mean, as caricatures of it sometimes represent it as meaning, that a man is saved against his will. No, it means that a man's will itself is renewed. His act of faith by which he is united to the Lord Jesus Christ is his own act. He performs that act gladly, and is sure that he never was so free as when he performs it. Yet he is enabled to perform it simply by the gracious, sovereign act of the Spirit of God.

Ah, my friends, how precious is that doctrine of the

grace of God! It is not in accordance with human pride. It is not a doctrine that we should ever have evolved. But when it is revealed in God's Word, the hearts of the redeemed cry, Amen. Sinners saved by grace love to ascribe not some but all of the praise to God.

Index of Names and Subjects

Index of Biblical References